# Publish Your Patterns!

## How To Write, Print, and Market Your Designs

Nancy Restuccia

Published by Make It Easy Sewing & Crafts™
A QuiltWoman.com company
26540 Canada Way, Carmel, CA 93923-9551
www.make-it-easy.com

Edited by Ann Anderson

Design and typography by Nancy Restuccia

**Publisher's Cataloging-in-Publication**
    *(Provided by Quality Books, Inc.)*

Restuccia, Nancy.
    Publish your patterns! : how to write, print, and
market your designs / by Nancy Restuccia. — 1st ed.
    p. cm.
    Includes index.
    ISBN: 0-9714501-3-7

    1. Handicraft—Design—Authorship.
    2. Self-publishing.   I. Title.

    TT149.R47 2002                   808'.066745
                                     QBI01-201257

# Dedication

To Ann and to Julia.
Without your support and encouragement, this book
would never have seen the light of day.

# Acknowledgements

I want to thank my professional colleagues and good friends for their incredible generosity in helping make this book far better than I could have on my own. Not only is this book better, but my life is richer for knowing them.

To my publisher and editor, Ann Anderson, for everything.

To my readers—Rosalie Cooke, Susan Huxley, Agnes Mercik, and Julia Pickett—for their perceptive comments and intelligent suggestions about organization as well as content. They are an impressive talent pool.

To my contributors—Ann Anderson, Patti Anderson, Rosalie Cooke, Jodie Davis, Beth Ferrier, Lois Fletcher, Daphne Greig, Mary-Jo McCarthy, and Susan Purney-Mark—for sharing their own experiences in the form of sidebars scattered throughout this book. Each adds valuable knowledge, and often a very different perspective, to my own thoughts and advice.

To Sylvia Landman, for sage advice regarding the title of this book.

And to the members of the Quilt Designers e-list for encouragement, inspiration, information, and fellowship over the years.

Thank you all!

# Table of Contents

# Foreword
# Fasten Your Seatbelts!

Publishing your own designs is a BLAST!

I've taken this journey before you, and I've learned a few things along the way. This book is my way of sharing that experience. I love sewing, quilting, and crafting, so I try to do whatever I can to help these wonderfully creative life-skills to flourish. I firmly believe that talented designers—particularly small independent designers—are the lifeblood of our industry.

And that is the perspective offered in these pages: that of a small, independent designer. Not amateur, mind you, simply small-scale and personal. There is a big difference.

My hope is to spare you many of the skinned knees and nosebleeds that are common on the self-publishing path, so you can do the important stuff better and reach your goals faster than I did.

Ready for take-off?

## What This Book Is About

Strictly speaking, publishing means getting a design from your head onto paper. That includes coming up with the idea, writing how-to instructions, creating a cover, delivering files to the printer, and packing patterns into bags. Section I, "From Idea to Paper," covers these steps in detail.

Why would you want to do all that?

Most people want to make at least a small profit from selling their patterns. Some folks do it mostly for fun—perhaps to share their designs, promote their craft, or for the satisfaction of seeing their name in print. Others might publish patterns to enhance their professional reputation and credibility. Teachers, for instance, might be willing to lose a little money on patterns in order to make more from their main business. Still others hope to earn a full-time living publishing a line of patterns. It's a very broad spectrum.

Whether your goal is to publish patterns as a sideline or a career, if profit figures into your personal equation, you'll want to read Section II, "The Marketing Approach." This section describes the five elements of the marketing mix—product, package, price, distribution, and advertising/publicity/promotion—and tells you how to use them to maximize your sales.

For those who hope to make pattern-publishing a full-time career, check out Section III, "Business & Legal Issues." It includes advice for setting up and running a business, including administration, finance, record keeping, and copyright registration.

Section IV, "Appendices," contains a variety of information. Appendix A is an explanation of two other ways to get your designs published (fee-for-service and royalty arrangements). Appendices B through J list many different resources, from trade publications to distributors to printers. Finally, Appendix K includes information about the folks who contributed sidebars to this book.

## Why Should You Take My Advice?

I founded and operated a pattern business from 1995 through 2001 called Make It Easy Sewing & Crafts®. During the years I operated it, I built my business from a single pattern to a line of seven, and from a negligible income to over $30,000 per year. So I know first-hand how to self-publish patterns and make a reasonable profit doing so. The best part, of course, is earning money doing something you absolutely love!

I'll cite examples from that business more than once in these pages. I sold Make It Easy in 2001 because it had grown so big, so fast, that I couldn't keep up with it myself and I didn't want to hire employees. That decision was based on a very personal preference. Many of you will hire employees when you get to that point and continue to grow your businesses until they become global empires. I'll warn you now: You may need another book for that part of your journey!

# Section I:

# From Idea to Paper

# Chapter 1
# The Idea

Most likely you've already got an idea for a pattern, and that's why you're reading this book. But whether you do or don't, every pattern starts with an idea. So I'll offer some thoughts on where they come from.

I find inspiration all around me. I draw on what I see; for instance in stores, catalogs, on the street, and at sewing, quilting, and craft shows. The spark of an idea may come from something I hear; for instance people talking on-line, at local guild meetings, and sending me email with ideas they'd like to see. Or from something I've done; for instance what the kids liked best during my years as a Girl Scout leader and classroom volunteer. And also from what I read; for instance in magazines and books. Good ideas are all around you, if you are on the lookout for them.

I keep files of projects that might make good patterns or articles. My files are full of magazine clippings, sketches, quotes—anything and everything that seems related to a single idea. Keeping "sparks" together this way helps a particular project to either (1) coalesce and become a pattern or article, or (2) prove the idea unworthy of further development. While it takes some discipline to maintain such files, they're a rich resource for inspiration when you're wondering what to do next.

## It's Not the Idea That's Hard

The difficult part of creating patterns isn't coming up with the idea. Let's be honest; you have at least one million-dollar idea in your head right now, right?

The difficult part is everything else that has to be done for an idea to see the light of day as a pattern. Will other people want to make the project? Will you be able to write instructions that are easy enough for people to follow? Are the materials readily available? Are there other patterns like yours? And if so, what makes yours different and better? Will you be able to sell enough to recoup your expenses and make a profit? And on and on. These are often tough questions.

The stew of ideas for my Humbug Bag™ pattern, for instance, was in a folder for ten years before I decided to make it a pattern. Every time I considered the folder I thought, "It's so easy, why would anyone buy this pattern?" So I moved on to the next folder.

Now I know that lots of people like to have explicit instructions even for simple projects. Plus I added value to a basic bag-form by including original extras like instructions for quilting and photocopy-ready gift tags. Those goodies gave me a point-of-difference versus my competition. All together, they've helped to make Humbug Bag a best-seller.

## Exploring the Concept

Once you've got an idea, it's time to play. (Yes, this is a legitimate part of your job, both time and materials. And if it's a business rather than a hobby, your supplies are tax-deductible. Don't ya just love it?)

Make the project. Then make it again, varying materials and techniques. And then make it again.

I typically make a dozen samples in different sizes, shapes, colors, embellishments, etc., before deciding on a final design. And then I figure out the best and quickest and easiest way to engineer *that* one by making a half dozen more.

Sometimes in this process, I discover that the project is too difficult or costly or requires too-obscure supplies to be viable as a pattern. In that case, it goes on the back burner to simmer or sink into oblivion. And I work on another idea.

# Chapter 2
# Writing Instructions

Ah, the "guts" of your pattern!

I used to think the instructions were the most important part of producing a quality pattern. And they probably are, in the long run. But what I quickly found out when I started selling patterns is that good instructions don't matter a hoot—at least not in making the first sale.

I was astounded at my first Quilt Market: Retailers, attracted by the sample hanging in the booth, asked to see the pattern cover. Only the cover. They had no interest in looking at my instructions, even when I offered. What they understood (and I do now, too) is that their customers will only look at a pattern if the cover does an exceptional job of selling itself.

Despite the importance of the cover at getting a customer's attention, the instructions are key to getting repeat business and establishing a good reputation in the long run. So make your instructions the best you possibly can: complete, accurate, and easy to follow. Deliver on those three promises, and you'll earn word-of-mouth advertising that will boost your sales with neither effort nor expenditure on your part. That kind of advertising is priceless.

## Know Your Limits

This needs to be said, and I apologize in advance if it hurts: Just because you can design and make a great project, that doesn't mean you can write, illustrate, and design a great pattern. Talented designers who are not great writers/illustrators/print designers should take justifiable pride in their creative ability, and then either hire out or educate themselves to do the rest of it. Some of the best designers in the world can't write a comprehensible how-to to save their life. But that's okay; their special talent is in designing, at which they excel.

If you fall into this category, check out the resources in the Appendices for help in those areas where you need it. Chances are you will make a better reputation and earn more money in the long run by paying someone to do well what you don't, than to stumble through and end up with an inferior product.

That said, I think almost anyone can produce clear, complete, and accurate instructions by following a rigorous process of making, testing, and revising.

## Overview of the Process

Over the years, I've come up with a process for writing instructions that ensures my patterns are as error-free and easy-to-follow as possible:

- Start by physically making the project, making careful how-to notes and detailed sketches as you go. Be sure to record the amounts of fabric and all tools and supplies that you need in a separate materials list.

- Take your notes to the computer and turn them into step-by-step words and illustrations. Make it as clear and complete as you can. Print yourself a copy.

- Take this first draft back to the studio. Cut yourself the exact amount of fabric(s) you specify in your materials list, and give yourself just those supplies you recommend. Then follow your instructions exactly, keeping thorough notes about where you left something out, got something wrong, weren't clear, came up short on fabric or supplies, etc.

- Go back to the computer for a second draft... and then back to the studio to test those revised instructions... and repeat as many times as necessary to get a draft that you think is perfect.

- Give that "perfect" draft (and the cover mock-up; see next chapter) to three or four testers—people who've never seen it before—and ask them to follow your instructions. That's how you'll find out all the mistakes you've become blind to by sheer over-exposure, and all the wording that seemed clear to you but completely baffles the rest of the thinking world.

- Eat an entire Sara Lee cheesecake, or a box of Godiva chocolates, or—my personal favorite—a pint of Ben & Jerry's Pistachio Pistachio ice cream. Then revise the instructions again, incorporating all your testers' comments to come up with the final, really perfect, set of instructions.

- Perfect... except for the two additional typos that will be brought to your attention by customers, teachers, and/or shop owners two months from now—generally on the day after you've picked up 5,000 copies from the printer.

Yes, writing how-to instructions for your pattern is that easy!

## Equipment and Programs

Let me quote the prolific and talented Trudie Hughes—author, designer, and quilt-shop owner:

"Advice to someone wanting to design: If you are planning to self-publish, by all means get good computer programs: good page-layout programs and especially good graphics programs. As a shop owner, I hate buying patterns with crummy layouts and poor illustrations. If you want to swim with the big fish, you have to look professional."

I'll second that.

Of course, that's if you want to sell to the mass market. If your target market is more limited, you can get away with less technology. Designers with a flair for hand-writing and drawing can even produce a pattern without a computer. But if you want to make publishing patterns your business, you need to seriously consider appropriate hardware and software.

Many would-be designers object that they don't have the money or time for decent equipment and software. They say they'll just make-do until their business volume justifies the expense of good tools. But if you were going into business as a carpenter, you wouldn't show up for work with a big rock rather than a hammer, would you? If you were going into business as a surgeon, you'd invest in a scalpel, not settle for a steak knife, right? The same logic applies to self-publishing patterns: To do a professional job, you need professional equipment and programs. It's an investment in your future.

Okay, end of sermon. What will you need to do it right? (Note: You can generally rent computers and the appropriate software at places like Kinkos if you're not ready to buy.)

First, you'll need a computer. Mac (the choice of the majority of commercial printers) or PC; either can do the job.

You'll also need one or more office printers: a laser- or inkjet printer for proofing your copy and illustrations; a bigger/faster laserprinter if you plan to print pattern instructions yourself; and a good quality color printer if you plan to print color covers or photos yourself. (Printing color covers yourself can be tricky; see page 39, "Color Printer Approach.")

And you'll need good computer programs. I use four types for my patterns:

- Word processing, for writing and editing text (I use Microsoft Word) [Note: Of these four, word-processing is the first one I'd give up; you can write directly into a page-layout program; and while editing is awkward, it is possible.]

- Drawing, for line drawings and diagrams (I use Macromedia FreeHand; Adobe Illustrator and CorelDRAW are other good ones) [Note: These type programs can be cajoled into doing acceptable page-layouts, if budget prohibits PageMaker or QuarkXPress; but they're far from the optimal choice.]

- Image editing, for tweaking photos and adding special backgrounds and effects (I use Adobe Photoshop) [Note: This is a sophisticated program; if photo-manipulation is not your thing, you might want to simply hire your printer or a digital-graphics expert to prep your images for print.]

- Page layout, for assembling all the above elements into a finished document ready for the printer (I use Adobe PageMaker and InDesign; QuarkXpress is another popular choice). Personally, I consider a page-layout program a necessity.

A note about specific programs. If you plan to use a commercial printer, check to see which programs they support. In general, today's print-industry standards are the programs cited above. But if you have a preference for a particular printer, you may want to invest in the same software they are most capable of supporting.

You may also want to invest in:

- Bar-code generator, for creating your UPC art (Universal Product Code); some drawing programs include this feature, such as CorelDRAW

- Adobe Acrobat, for creating PDFs (Portable Document Format; theoretically, a universally readable file format that maintains original scale; useful, for instance, if you want to offer downloadable documents on your Web site); some page-layout programs come with this installed, such as PageMaker and InDesign

- Web-site software, if you want to create and maintain your own Web site

- And if you are publishing quilting patterns, CAD (Computer Aided Design) programs such as EQ (Electric Quilt) and Quilt-Pro are worth considering. They allow you to play with designs and color schemes, and also to create class handouts. But please, don't publish a pattern based only on an EQ or Quilt-Pro design; do actually make the block and quilt!

Before purchasing a program, check at your community college to see if you can sit in on a few classes to see which of the programs suit you best. Ultimately it's a question of what works best for you and what fits your budget.

## *General Tips for Writing Instructions*

### Format

- Take a look at other patterns. Try to put into words what makes one good and the other not so good. If you find one you think is exceptional, model your own on it.

- Use words and pictures. Different people learn in different ways. Some people learn best from pictures, and others from words.

  When I write a pattern, I write and illustrate it so that a verbal-learner can read the words and come up with a great finished project; and a visual-learner can follow the illustrations and end up with the same successful result. Many people will consult both words and pictures, of course. A good rule-of-thumb when deciding whether an illustration is needed is: Can someone who is just looking at the pictures get the whole story?

- Organize your instructions into logical sections, and then into discrete steps. For instance, if your pattern is for making a doll, one section might be "The Face," which includes step-by-step detail how to stitch or draw features. A quilt pattern might have a section "Add the Borders" with step-by-step measurement, cutting, and stitching details.

  By doing this, you break down the entire process into digestible chunks. It helps your customer to organize his/her time, and also

to understand how each step fits into the whole. (Look at the way this book is broken into small chunks through the use of chapters, heads, subheads, bullet points, and sidebars. Isn't that easier to understand than a solid string of text?)

- Keep the eye-scan-length of your text within easy-to-read bounds. In other words, if you're printing your instructions on an 8½″×11″ sheet, break it into two columns. It's impossible to easily scan text that spans an entire letter-size page. Four inches is about the limit for easily readable text.

- Be consistent. If you use 1.25″ one place, don't use 1¼″ somewhere else. If you use "on-line," don't use "online" later. If you use 14-point bold type for your first subhead, also use it for your second, third, and fourth.

I use a two-part form to maintain consistency, illustrated on the next two pages.

Part 1 is a two-page form; page-one is shown at right and page-two is described in the caption. In Part 1, I note my standards for words, phrases, punctuation, format, etc. For example, for this book, in the box labeled "C-D-E" I noted "CorelDRAW." Under "I-J-K-L" I reminded myself to search and replace "info" with "information." Under "W-X-Y-Z" I wrote "yards, not yds." Under "Punctuation," I noted "serial commas." (A serial comma is one after the second-to-last item in a list. For instance, "lions, tigers and bears" does not use a serial comma; "lions, tigers, and bears" does.) In the "Numbers" box, I wrote "fractions, not decimals."

A portion of my Part 2 Style Sheet for this book is reproduced on page 20. Part 2 details type and page styles. This may not be necessary for a short pattern or instruction sheet; but for longer publications, it is invaluable to maintain consistency.

### Choosing & Editing Your Words

- Use parallel construction in writing your steps. That makes it much easier for your customer to understand and follow along.

| Style Sheet, Part 1, for: | | Page 1 |
|---|---|---|
| A-B | C-D-E | F-G-H |
| I-J-K-L | M-N | O-P-Q |

*Part 1, page one, of a typical style sheet for common words, phrases, and usages (reduced to fit page; actual form is full-sheet).*

*The six boxes on page two are labelled "R-S," "T-U-V," "W-X-Y-Z," "Punctuation," "Numbers," and "Miscellaneous."*

## Type/Page Styles for *Publish Your Patterns!*

**TYPE STYLES:**

Chapter #:

  Helvetica, 18/21.6

  ¶: 0.056 (p4) after, keep with next, center, pagebreak before

  Hyphenation off

Chapter Title:

  Mona Lisa Solid ITC TT, 36/auto

  ¶: 0.167 (p12) after, keep with next, center

  Hyphenation off

Head:

  Helvetica BoldItalic, 13.5/auto

  ¶: 0.167 (p12) before, 0.083 (p6) after, keep with next, left

  Hyphenation off

Subhead:

  Helvetica Bold, 12.5/auto

  ¶: 0.167 (p12) before, 0.056 (p4) after, keep with next, left

  Hyphenation off

Body text:

  AGaramond, 11/13.2

  ¶: 1st indent 0.333, 0.028 (p2) after, left

Sidebar title:

  Mona Lisa Solid ITC TT, 16/17

  ¶: 0.83 (p6) after, keep with next, center

  Hyphenation off

Sidebar byline:

  AGaramond Italic, 12.5/auto

  ¶: 0.111 (p8) after, keep with next, center

  Hyphenation off

Caption:

  AGaramond Italic, 11/12

  ¶: 0.056 (p4 ) after, keep with next, center

  Hyphenation off

**PAGE STYLES:**

Margins:

  Top, 1.25

  Outside, 1.25

  Inside, 1.5

  Bottom, 1.0

Columns: two, space between 0.16

*Part 2 of style sheet, used to record type-style and page-layout standards*

Personally, I like to start each step with a verb because verbs imply action. I want my customers to feel energized and enthused to make the project. (Take a look at the pattern excerpt, next page; each bulleted step begins with a verb. That's parallel construction.)

• Choose short rather than long words and sentences for most effective communication.

• Write concisely; edit heartlessly. Rather than, "Be sure that you measure and double-check that your seam allowance is just a quarter-inch" say "Stitch, using a ¼″ seam allowance." Get rid of articles (like "the") whenever possible. For instance, instead of "cut the fabric" say "cut fabric."

## Content

• Include complete, easy-to-follow instructions.

Have you seen the Sidney Harris cartoon of the two scientists, in which one has drawn an elaborate mathematical formula on a blackboard—all "$\pi$"s and "$\Sigma$"s and "$\sqrt{}$"s?

## 4. Add ribbon and stitch top edge:

**a.** Unzip zipper. (Bag is still inside out.)

**b.** Thread jingle bell onto ribbon and slide to center, keeping ribbon untwisted. *Tip:* Trim ribbon end to sharp point for easiest threading.

**c.** Bring ribbon ends together; center them on the pin-mark at top edge of fabric, with raw ends barely extending beyond fabric edge; pin ribbon in place.

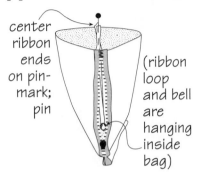

center ribbon ends on pin-mark; pin

(ribbon loop and bell are hanging inside bag)

**d.** Pinch the top of the zipper and the pinned ribbon ends together. Holding these two match-points firmly (or pin if desired), align raw edges and stitch across top, ½" from fabric edge. *Tip:* Flatten bottom of bag to make working with top edge easier.

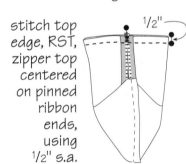

stitch top edge, RST, zipper top centered on pinned ribbon ends, using ½" s.a.

½"

## 5. Finish:

**a.** Serge-finish seam allowances at top and bottom, using a three- or four-thread wide overedge stitch. If you don't have a serger, zigzag or overedge using your conventional machine.

**b.** Secure thread ends (use seam sealant or tuck serger tails into the seam allowance).

**c.** Turn bag right side out.

**d.** Tie gift tag to hole in zipper pull.

*Excerpt from Humbug Bag™ pattern, reprinted with permission.*

*This example shows most of the points made in this chapter, for instance: instructions are formatted in narrow, easy-to-read columns; each step is written with parallel construction (i.e., they all start with a verb); illustrations are clear and explanatory on their own; the typeface is large enough to be readable; instructions are broken into managable bites; consistency is maintained; etc.*

Between the equation and the answer, the scientist has written the phrase, "Then a miracle occurs." Unfortunately, a lot of small-press patterns suffer from this same problem: the assumption that customers will be able to miraculously get from step 3 to 4, even though the pattern doesn't tell how.

• On the other hand, don't get carried away. Remember, this is a pattern not an encyclopedia. It's a fine balance, but one worth walking thoughtfully. Use the skill-level of your target consumer as a guide. If you're writing for advanced quilters, you don't need to include an explanation of how to hold a rotary cutter; they know that. But if your pattern is targeted toward beginners, it's probably appropriate to tell them what a rotary cutter is as well as how to use it. Teachers and shop-owners can often answer your questions in this regard.

• For garment patterns, make sure sections that are intended to be sewn together are indeed the same length, that notches match up, and that "mileposts" such as grainlines, center-front, center-back, waistline, etc., are clearly marked to facilitate pattern adjustments.

# Make It Right!

## The Importance of Accurate and Complete

*by Rosalie Cooke, editor of **Art You Wear** newsletter*

A popular feature of my newsletter is the pattern reviews. I'm committed to giving my readers an honest evaluation and to helping solve possible problems in the pattern. Because I thoroughly read and test so many patterns, I offer the following personal opinions:

People may buy your patterns a first time, but you endanger future sales if you frustrate the consumer. If pattern pieces are missing, if seams don't match, or if the finished pattern doesn't look like the cover, you will upset customers. I don't think the world's most original, exquisite designs will sell well if consumers can't reproduce what they imagined when they bought the patterns. If you sabotage their dream, you lose. If customers make "wadders" that end up in the trash, you have failed as much as they did. Help them. Save yourself and your customers the aggravation: Check your pattern pieces and write directions so clear and complete that there's little chance of misunderstanding.

How? Test your pattern with both experienced sewing friends and the timid beginner who is unsure of her skills. If she can figure out the pattern, be happy. If she makes mistakes, study them and improve what you've produced.

I commend the pattern designers who encourage creativity by offering suggestions for variations. But most of us don't enjoy being forced into improvisation via errors. We also can't handle the "go for it and be creative, we'll just give you the bare bones" approach. We need a solid foundation to start with. Tell us exactly how you made the original. Even the experienced like clear instructions—don't assume they can figure it out on their own. Poor drafting or instructions come across as sloppy or even unskilled and unprofessional pattern design.

Did you know that people spread the word farther, wider, and faster if they are unhappy with a product than if they like it? Why risk your good name and reputation? Need I mention it definitely will affect your bank account? On a positive note, let me assure you that when I find a complete, well-written pattern, I definitely tell everyone about it!

---

- Think about whether to cite measurements in imperial (e.g., inches) and/or metric (e.g., centimeters) units. To cover all the global bases, use both.

- Be accurate! This is one of the most important rules for a successful pattern. If you can afford it, hire a professional editor. And absolutely, positively, ask three or more people to test your pattern: to actually make it and comment on clarity, accuracy, etc. Lots more on editors and testers later in this chapter.

## Type

- Choose a typeface and size that is easy to read. Avoid quirky, funky, highly stylized faces, except for titles and chapter heads, where they can add sparkle to your text.

- According to research, serif type is more readable than sans serif in extended text blocks. ("Serifs" are the little crosshatches added to the main strokes of type. This paragraph is serif; the subhead "Type," above, is sans serif.)

Research also shows that aligning text blocks "flush left" (also called "ragged right") is easier to read than "justified" type (text that is even on both left and right sides). This copy is aligned flush left; the paragraph in the tint box at right is justified.

- Choose a typeface that reinforces the image of your project. Typefaces have "personality." E.g., Schoolbook (this paragraph) has a "See Spot run" feel to it. Garamond (next paragraph) feels elegant.

- Use typographic standards rather than typewriter conventions for a professional look. These include using:

  > "smart quotes" (the ones that curve, as in this text) rather than "tick marks" (the straight up-and-down ones)

  > an "em-dash" (—) rather than two hyphens (--) for a dash

  > one space, not two, between sentences

- For measurements, use primes or at least tick marks rather than smart quotes (i.e., 5′3″ or 5'3", respectively; not 5'3"). Prime marks and other special characters are typically "hidden" on your keyboard, accessed by multi-key-combinations. (For instance, Option + Shift + underline gives me the em-dash on my Mac.) Check your manual or on-line help to find these special characters.

An exceptional reference book for these and more typographical rules is *Type It Right! the little black book for your computer*, by Anita Stumbo. (See Appendix J for details.)

## *Other Things To Include*

### Commercial-Production Disclaimer

Inevitably, you'll get requests from customers asking for permission to make items using your pattern, to sell at craft fairs and the like. Include an explanation of your policy.

You may be delighted for customers to make and sell all they want. Or you may decide that since they're making a profit from

your work, they should compensate you for your contribution to their success.

My own approach is a compromise:

> Purchase of this pattern entitles you to make as many (pattern name) as you like for your personal use, including to give as gifts. Purchase of this pattern also entitles you to make up to (twelve or twenty-four, generally) items per year to sell at bazaars and craft fairs. If you're interested in selling larger volumes, please write or call for information on purchasing a commercial license.

This note serves an educational purpose as well, letting customers know that profiting from someone else's work isn't an unlimited right. (More about licenses in Chapter 15.)

## Copyright Warning

Another element you should include in your instructions is a clear explanation of your copyright. In my experience, most consumers are happy to comply once they understand the rules. Again, this note serves an educational purpose as well as a legal warning.

The words I typically include somewhere on each page (usually in the footer) are:

> © 2002 Nancy Restuccia. All Rights Reserved. Written permission is required to copy and/or distribute copies of this page, whether or not you profit from it.

That final clause—"whether or not you profit from it"—is particularly important, in my opinion. Many people think that if they give away rather than sell copies of a pattern, that's okay. The problem, of course, is that by doing so they are depriving the designer of her fair profit. And that's why it's illegal.

Another phrase I sometimes include is:

> Photocopying, digitizing, and all other copying to "share" these instructions is strictly prohibited by law. Thank you for respecting the designer's copyright.

(Call me paranoid or pedantic if you want, but I do believe that education is the answer to most of our copyright problems. We all need to do our part to educate consumers—gently and respectfully, of course.)

Finally, if your pattern includes things that you *want* your customer to copy (e.g., foundations for quilt blocks, the design for a doll's face), then note that permission is given to do so. Copy shops often enforce copyright, and your customer will be annoyed if they are not allowed to photocopy what they need to make the pattern. My Humbug Bag™ pattern, for instance, contains the note:

> Purchase of this pattern grants you permission to photocopy the next page to make gift tags for your Humbug Bags.

## Contact Information

Let customers know how to get in touch with you if they have problems or questions about your pattern.

Be pleasant, attentive, and sincere when a customer calls or emails with a problem. Thank her for letting you know about it, and help her to solve it. Afterwards, consider whether other customers are likely to have the same problem. If so, correct the pattern.

Offer to send those who've purchased an incorrect pattern a corrected page, or even an entirely fresh pattern. If it's a minor correction, you can notify customers via email. Taking the initiative to correct errors will earn you good-will that will be repaid many times over in word-of-mouth advertising.

## *Editors*

Many designers assume their testers will edit their pattern. This is not a good assumption. Editors and testers do different jobs.

A professional editor can do any or all of the following: correct spelling and grammar; eliminate wordiness; catch where your text and illustrations are out of synch (e.g., your text says "stitch right sides together" but your illustration indicates that wrong sides are stitched together); double-check references (e.g., phone numbers and book titles), measurements, and calculations; identify inconsistencies (e.g., the same word spelled differently, such as "gray" and "grey"); and offer suggestions for organizing your information more understandably. Understand upfront what it is you are hiring an editor to do.

With so many flawed patterns on the market today, it can enhance your pattern's value to add a cover credit, "Edited by (well-respected editor)." This let's potential customers know that you've taken great care to provide a quality product. Appendix B lists a number of editors whose integrity and quality I can personally vouch for.

## *Testers*

Testers make up the project from your pattern final-draft and let you know whether they enjoyed it, found it frustrating, couldn't follow something, ran out of fabric, couldn't locate the required supplies, etc. They're your guinea pigs. Their job is to warn you of problems you don't even suspect, so you can fix them before releasing the pattern to a wider audience.

## Who?

Testers should be representative of the type of person you expect your pattern to appeal to. If your pattern is for beginners, your testers should include beginners, too. (You might want to include at least one tester of a different experience level, in case you've misjudged your pattern.)

I aim for a variety of personality types among my testers. People come in a huge range of flavors. Different types will react differently to the same pattern. For instance, a perfectionist who follows instructions to a T will almost certainly have a very different reaction than a slap-dash free-spirit type. A young and an older person often have different perspectives. A shop owner will view a pattern differently from a plain-vanilla consumer. All these points of view are valuable.

I find many of my testers on email lists (such as those sponsored by Quiltropolis and Yahoo Groups). These are people I've gotten to know over the course of six months or a year, whose general personality, integrity, and knowledge I can gauge. As a rule, I don't use people I don't know to test my patterns. It's like a movie review: You can't judge whether the information is any good if you don't know the source.

## Timing

I normally give testers from ten days to three weeks to finish their review, depending on the project. Most of them make the project the day before it's due. Be clear when asking that they know the timing and can meet your deadline, so you don't get caught having to go to print with an untested pattern.

## To Pay or Not to Pay

My own philosophy regarding testing is to neither pay nor provide materials to testers, for three reasons:

- Paying them could influence them to say better things than they otherwise might.

- By supplying materials, you automatically disallow them the opportunity to make the project out of all sorts of inappropriate stuff they have hanging around. Quite often, this is excellent information that you'd never come upon yourself.

- By requiring testers to gather materials, you find out whether they understood the requirements, whether supplies were difficult to find, whether they considered them too expensive, etc. That's information I want to know before going to print.

I don't require my testers to make the project if, once they see the pattern, they are disinterested or the materials are too expensive, etc. Their only obligation is to let me know why they didn't want to make it.

I have never been turned down by anyone because I didn't offer a cash payment. In fact, most people are delighted to test a pattern if it's even remotely interesting.

While I don't pay my testers in cash, I do pay them in recognition. I publicly thank them in the pattern. (Note: Confirm that they're okay having their name in print; some people prefer anonymity.) I also follow up with two copies of the pattern—one autographed, one not—and often some little gift to show my appreciation.

When I use other designers or writer friends as testers, I often offer an exchange: I'll test (or edit) one of theirs if they do one of mine. That's generally a very welcome payment.

## Put It In Writing

I'm not one for unnecessary formality. Even so, once a tester has agreed verbally, I put the details of my request in writing to minimize the possibility of misunderstandings. I confirm the project, timing, payment (credit rather than cash), and what I expect from them. A sample letter I used not too long ago follows on the next page; feel free to adapt it to your purpose.

## Send Paper, Not Pixels

It's tempting when you're up against a deadline to email your instructions to testers. If you're looking for a reaction to the information, but not the format, email may work fine.

However, if you want a reaction to words and format, send paper. That way you know exactly what your tester is looking at. Very often, digital files get changed in either the sending or the printing when they travel over the Internet. (Even PDFs, which theoretically should be exact duplicates of your file.) It's reassuring not to have to consider that complication when evaluating feedback.

Hi, Kay!

I've got a proposition: Would you be interested in testing my next pattern? It's called Humbug Bag™ and it's a quick and easy little bag, can but doesn't have to be made of quilted fabric. I would send you a reasonably-good draft of the instructions and cover, and you would either:

- Make the project and comment on the instructions, noting particular problems or opportunities for improvement

- React to the pattern by saying, "Yuck! I have no interest in ever making this, what *is* that woman thinking?!"

In either event, I'd like to get your overall impressions and reasons for liking or not liking it—within about 10 days if possible. (This particular project should take no more than two hours, start to finish; I can make one in 20 minutes; but then, I've been practicing.)

To keep this from having any tinge of bribery, I'm sorry I can't offer you payment to do this; I'm asking it as a favor, and hoping that it will be fun for you, too. Your reward is a free pattern, autographed and with many thanks, when it's hot off the presses—and of course, my undying gratitude.

Any interest? I should have a draft ready to send middle of next week, so I'd want to get comments back by the end of the month at the latest. If you're willing, please let me know your mailing address so I can send you the pattern.

Thanks for considering this,


Nancy Restuccia

*Sample letter to prospective pattern tester*

# Chapter 3
# The Cover

The cover sells your first pattern. The instructions keep customers coming back for more. Both are important for long-term success. But you'll never even get off the ground if you don't get the cover right from the start.

## Cover Model(s) & Composition

Your cover photo has to say it all, in one universally representative and appealing image. Which *one* image will do the best job?

Tough to choose. You want to appeal to the widest audience. But some people like blue and others red. Should you use this year's "hot" colors? Or will that outdate your pattern next year when something else is the color *du jour*?

And what about fabrics and motifs? Should you use country plaids or contemporary batiks? Should you feature the squirrel or the moose appliqué? The list goes on and on. How do you decide what will be most appealing?

My very scientific answer is: Go with your gut. Well, that and a little research.

One of the benefits of making your project again and again while testing your instructions (see previous chapter) is that you can experiment with different colors, textures, design concepts, etc., to see what works best. In the end, it's a personal decision. But that's a big part of what you offer as a designer: your unique vision. Don't be afraid to make a statement. If the chartreuse model screams, "Pick me!," go for it.

Of course, it never hurts to do some research to confirm your gut feeling. Ask friends which of your variations they'd personally most like to own. Ask teachers and shop owners; they often have a good perspective on what appeals broadly to consumers. Still, I think it's a mistake to cater completely to market demand. Let your unique vision shine through; it adds energy to your presentation.

### Free Fabric, Etc.

A note on free fabric, notions, etc. Some manufacturers have programs to encourage designers to use their products in cover models or to include them in the list of materials. Fabric companies often offer "designer cuts" of new lines, before the fabrics reach stores.

The best place to approach manufacturers is at a trade show. Simply attending, or better yet, having a booth at a trade show tells manufacturers that you are serious about your business.

### Composition

If your pattern is for making one item, composing the photo is easy: That one item is the focus. Make it as big and as close-up as possible so consumers can see the detail they need in order to decide to buy. As a rule, show variations—different color schemes, for instance—as small "thumbnail" photos.

Cover composition gets trickier if your pattern includes more than one project. My Jambalaya™ pattern, for instance, includes instructions for making four different wall quilts. For the cover, I created a collage of the four, each one the same size. The result was that the entire photo was plenty big, but each quilt was too small to make a big impact from a display rack. Plus, the image was so complex it tended to be confusing. In retrospect, the cover photo should have been just one of the

quilts (the most popular) printed big, with the other three as thumbnails alongside it. In fact, that's what I did for subsequent advertising, and it was indeed a more attention-grabbing image. Again, we learn.

## *Photo or Illustration?*

Either can work, if it shows enough detail that the customer knows what they're buying. With garment patterns, people want to know where the seams are, how full the garment is, etc. With quilts, customers want to see how complicated the piecing and quilting are.

In my experience, it is more difficult to come up with a winning illustration than a photo. So while I don't discount that an illustration can work (especially for garment patterns) I'll focus here on cover photos, which I believe increase the odds for success for most sewing, quilting, and craft patterns.

## *Hire a Professional*

The #1 reason a buyer (retail, wholesale, and distributor) passes on a pattern is a poor cover photo or illustration—too small, poor quality, can't see details, unappealing colors, etc. That's why I recommend using a professional photographer. While the cost may seem high, remember that if your photo is not great, you might as well not print any patterns because no one will buy them. (Costs are generally in the $300–$600 range for half a day of shooting, which will get you one to four usable shots.)

### Digital or Film?

A digital file is preferred by most printers, and will likely be faster and less expensive for you, particularly if you use direct-to-plate technology. (Digital technology is changing quickly. While a professional digital camera is in a class by itself, some of the better consumer models can produce an image that will work for a standard pattern cover.)

A digital image has the added advantage that you can adjust it on the computer, for instance to replace the background, add drop-shadows, and tweak colors (Adobe Photoshop is the program of choice for this). And you can audition different sizes and crops in your pattern layout, so you don't have to guess what your cover will look like when printed.

### Digital Considerations

With digital, your finished "photo" will be a file on a computer disk rather than a slide or transparency. You'll need to tweak the photo for printing; i.e., adjust for color, brightness, contrast, etc. If you know Photoshop *and* you know print, you can do this yourself. If you are not familiar with prepping a file for print, hire an expert to do it for you (your printer may do this, or ask them for a recommendation).

Know the finished size of your photo. The digital file will be prepped for printing at a specific finished size. If you're not exactly sure, better to estimate a little big than small. Try not to be off by more than about 20%. Sizing a photo up or down more than that can significantly compromise image quality.

### Film Considerations

Film can be used directly by your printer (just draw a box labeled "for placement only" on your cover layout, indicating where the photo goes); or it can be converted to a digital file so you can manipulate the image as described above.

A professional photographer will ask what film format you need. For 5½″×8½″ pattern covers, 35mm is usually adequate for capturing good detail. If you need a larger image—an 8½″×11″ book cover, for instance—choose 2¼″ format. And if you're planning to print large posters, ask for a 4″×5″ transparency.

## Arrive at the Studio Prepared

To keep studio time (and thus cost) to a minimum, arrive prepared: Know how you want your models and props arranged, the finished photo size, and what color background you want. Most photographers will have an assortment of "seamless" papers to choose from for background color. If you intend your final image to "float" on the page rather than be contained within a frame, choose a color that is the same color as the paper you will print on—typically white.

Bring a cover mock-up to the photo shoot. Use your home digital camera to capture the arrangement you like best, and use it to create your mock-up. Seeing a mock-up helps the photographer understand what the shot needs to convey and how it fits on the page. He or she may have suggestions regarding arrangement and/or cropping and/or lighting that will enhance your finished cover.

Bring all necessary props. If you need help propping and arranging your shot, hire a stylist (your photographer can recommend one).

---

### Photo Propping Tips

In general, avoid props and complicated backdrops; they often confuse the consumer about what the pattern includes. On the other hand, it can be helpful to include a simple prop or two in order to convey finished size.

For instance, I included some coins and a lipstick in the photo of my Humbug Bag™—common objects that communicate the small scale of the bag without adding a question whether they're part of the pattern. But I also once used a baby quilt as a backdrop (for KinderKakes™, my first pattern). If I had a nickel for everyone who asked if that quilt was included in the pattern, I'd be a rich woman today. We learn.

---

## Taking Your Own Photo

If you decide to to take your own photos, shoot slides (ASA 100 or slower) rather than prints for the sharpest image. (This assumes that you will be converting it to a digital file for printing your cover. If you plan to glue an actual photo print to your covers, then shoot print film. See "Adhered Photo Approach" on pages 38–39.)

To get the best textural detail, use a "raking" light. In other words, set up both a frontal light source and one that angles-in sharply from one side or a corner. This casts enough shadow that texture shows up nicely, for instance in quilts. Consider buying or renting one to three 500W photo-flood light bulbs and fixtures/stands if you want strong, controllable light. (Don't put these bulbs in a regular lamp fixture; they're too hot.)

If you shoot outdoors (which can be very sweet light, even if unpredictable and uncontrollable), wait for a slightly overcast day or shoot in the morning or late afternoon. Bright direct sunlight tends to wash out details.

Then take your slides to a trustworthy, quality photo-processing shop and have them transferred to CD, so you (or someone you hire) can tweak the images for print.

## *Pattern Name*

Your pattern needs a name. And not just any name; a great name! One that is distinctive, fun, and memorable. One that captures the spirit of your project, entices consumers to grab it off the shelf, and stirs all the right feelings. A name that nobody else is using. Whew! That's a tall order.

Still, it can be done; and it's actually fun.

### Descriptive and Evocative Names

There are two basic approaches to naming patterns: descriptive and evocative.

A descriptive name is straightforward, e.g., Big Blue Bear for a denim teddy bear. The advantage of this approach is that the consumer knows exactly what you're selling. A name that includes a promise also falls into the descriptive category, e.g., The World's Easiest Quilt Pattern. Again, the consumer understands exactly what you're selling.

An evocative name can be either an existing word or phrase applied in an unexpected way (e.g., Jambalaya™), or it can be made up (e.g., Rumbleford™). The effect of an evocative title is to suggest a feeling. I thought Rumbleford suggested the feeling of old-time travel in a train or Model T. That was perfect for the product—an old-fashioned, hand-crafted, luxurious carry-on bag. Tide and Bounce are well-known examples of evocative product names.

Evocative names also includes nonsense words (e.g., DipDapDollies) and made-up words (e.g., Quiltasaurus, Craftropolis, Thimbleberries). This kind of name will take more work to build an identity around, but in the long run can be very effective.

## Other Considerations

Considerations in choosing a name:

- Is it easy to say?
- Is it easy to spell? (If customers are looking for you on the Web or in the phone book, don't confound them with odd spellings they are unlikely to anticipate.)
- Is it easy to remember?
- Does it mean something unflattering in another language? (Remember the car Nova? In Spanish, *no va* means doesn't go.)
- Is the name, or one similar, being used by someone in an industry you don't want to be associated with? (Legally you can use the same name as another business if it's in a different industry. However, if it's also the name of, say, a pesticide or toilet-bowl cleaner, you might not want that association. Of course, this is a matter of opinion.)
- Some people feel strongly about having a name that begins with "A" so they will be listed early in alphabetical directories.

## Is It Taken?

The biggest difficulty in coming up with a name is that many are already taken. Once you've got some possibilities, check whether they're available. Search thoroughly; you absolutely do not want to start using a name and then find that someone has already trademarked it. At best, you will have to change all your stationery and patterns; at worst, you'll end up in court for trademark infringement. Some places to check:

- Phone books
- The Web (search using several search engines; the results will vary)
- A Web domain-name registration service, such as www.networksolutions.com
- The U.S. Patent and Trademark Office searchable database on the Web at www.uspto.gov/web/menu/tm.html
- Your state business-licensing division (often the Secretary of State office)

Check variations of a name, too. If you are thinking of using DipDapDollies, check Dip Dap Dollies (one has spaces between words, the other doesn't) as well. If you like Quilt Sew Easy, also check Quilt So Easy.

A book that I found helpful is *Names That Sell: How to Create Great Names for Your Company, Product, or Service*, by Fred Barrett. (See Appendix J for details.)

Once you decide on a name, be sure to include the ™ symbol when you use it. That gives notice to others that you have claimed it as your trademark. See Chapter 15 for information on registering a trademark (the ® symbol means the mark is federally registered).

## Complete Materials List

Typically this is the major element on a pattern's back cover. It should include everything a customer needs to make the project: all materials as well as any supplies and equipment that are not sewing-room basics.

Having a complete materials list on the cover makes your pattern more appealing to all customers. It makes it easy for consumers to gather everything they need, so when the time comes to make the project they won't have to stop midway through and run to the store for a key ingredient. For your wholesale/distributor customers, a materials list can add value to

your product by helping them sell related items. This can be an important selling point for marketing your pattern to shops and teachers; it adds incremental sales and profit with little effort. So whenever a specialty item is necessary or desirable, specify it in your materials list.

## Specifying Fabric Amounts

The amount of fabric to specify in your materials list is a controversial measurement. In the U.S., most sew-ers don't give a second thought to purchasing more fabric than absolutely necessary, just in case. However in many other countries—for instance Australia—the price of fabric is so dear that consumers want to know the *exact* amount needed to complete a project; and then to decide for themselves whether to buy extra.

My own feeling is that it doesn't matter how you figure the numbers as long as customers understand what they mean. For instance, if you have allowed extra fabric for shrinkage, trimming selvages, and fixing goofs, tell them how much extra you added. If the amounts specified are exact minimums, let them know so they can add a fudge factor if they desire.

I used to think that giving an exact amount of fabric was good. After all, I personally always try to squeeze the most out of my yard goods. So I strove for "just enough" in writing my materials lists. Then a reviewer criticized my Jambalaya™ pattern because she had only just enough fabric. Yikes! That's what I was going for, and she wrote it up as if I had committed a sin. Now I clearly communicate my assumptions when specifying materials.

## A Word About Width

Shopkeepers generally agree that 42″ wide is the maximum width you should assume for off-the-bolt yardage these days for quilting-type fabrics. Personally I assume a 40″ usable width, to allow for shrinkage and trimming off selvages. But again, your assumptions are best specified in your materials list, so customers can make their own judgment. If your craft uses another type of fabric, ask at several stores what the standard is for width these days.

## Availability

Check that everything you're specifying in your materials list is widely available. Go to several stores, including national chains, to be sure you're not sending your customers on a snark hunt. (Note that availability is becoming less of a problem with the proliferation of Web-based stores.)

## *Designing Your Cover*

Your cover design doesn't have to be slick or fancy; some of the most successful pattern lines use a very straightforward design concept.

## Cover Template

Develop a template—a generic format—for your covers from the start, and follow it when designing all your patterns (see example at right). It not only makes your design job easier; it's also a valuable marketing tool, helping consumers pick out your patterns from among the many on the shelf.

To build awareness and reputation, your unique "look" should reinforce the image of your company. For instance, if the image you want to project is "cutting edge," then your graphics, typeface, colors, design, and writing style should communicate "cutting edge." If your image is "country," then all these elements should communicate "country."

Each of the elements included in the template at right is summarized below.

## Photo/Illustration

Your photo or illustration should be the focal point of the front cover. It should occupy at least a third of the space available; more if possible. Position it near the top of the front cover so it'll show if your pattern is displayed in a stacked rack.

Position additional photos (e.g., project made up in other colors, other projects based on the pattern) on front and/or back, clearly subordinate to the cover shot. Your cover needs a clear focal point, which is the main photo/illustration of your project.

## Pattern Name

Include the pattern name near the top of your front cover, too. If your company identity is more recognizable than the pattern name (e.g., Thimbleberries—and chances are if you're reading this book, you're not there yet), you might want the company rather than the pattern name in the top third.

## Item Number

For small companies, this is almost a laughable inclusion at first blush. You only have a few patterns and know them all by name, so why do you need a number? Because catalogs and distributors rely on code numbers for ordering and fulfillment. So print an item number on each pattern. In my experience, most customers use four- or five-digit order numbers.

## Project Finished Size

People like to know how big the thing they're making is going to be. Clearly state the finished size on your pattern cover.

## What's Included

Tell what's included in your pattern. Particularly note any extras or goodies that add to the pattern's value (e.g., gift tags, foundation papers, technique instructions). Also tell what's not included if there's any potential for confusion. For instance, if you show a variation—say, a table runner made with the quilt-pattern blocks—but you only include instructions for the wall quilt; or if you use a handcrafted prop or backdrop in your photo; make it clear that instructions for the variations are not included in the pattern.

#01734

# Great Name™

Spectacular photo
or illustration

Finished size: 22″x28″

*A catchy & compelling
characterizing phrase!*

A "teach-me-
how" pattern
(great for
beginners)

- Bullet points that tell what
  your pattern will deliver
  - Is it fun? Easy? Quick?
  - Easy to personalize? A good
    gift for men? Learn a new skill?
  - What makes your pattern
    stand out from the crowd?

*Edited by Rosalie Cooke*

**Make It Easy**®
SEWING & CRAFTS
A QuiltWoman.com Company

---

## Materials List

All materials, supplies, tools, and
equipment needed to make the
project (except for standard
sewing-room supplies)

Project done in
three other
colorways or styles

**Make It Easy**®
SEWING & CRAFTS
A QuiltWoman.com Company
26540 Canada Way
Carmel, CA 93923
Toll free 1-877-454-7967  Fax 831-624-7132
email: ann@quiltwoman.com
Web: www.make-it-easy.com

**UPC**

(a box 1 ³⁄₄″ x 2 ¹⁄₂″,
anchored to right and
bottom edges of pattern
back, is adequate space)

*Sample cover-design template for an 8½″×11″ printed page,
which will be folded once to a 5½″×8½″ cover.*

## Company Name/Contact Information

Include full identification—company name, logo, address, phone number(s), email address—everything a potential, dissatisfied, or satisfied customer needs to get in touch with you. Shops and teachers need to be able to reach you when a customer/student recommends your pattern to them. Consumers may need to call with a question, problem, or compliment. Make it easy for them. You especially don't want consumers complaining or asking questions of shopkeepers who simply resell your pattern.

Whether to include your Web-site URL is a bit controversial. Some folks believe that it is "advertising"; that by including it on your cover, you are in essence competing with retail stores for the same business. Others believe it is a service to your customers, allowing them to gain access to you personally in case of a question. This one is a difficult call; I leave it up to you. If you don't intend to sell your patterns through shops and distributors, by all means include your Web address.

## Universal Product Code (UPC)

If you want to mass-market patterns, a UPC is rapidly becoming a must rather than an option. Some distributors, for instance, only consider products that have a UPC.

A UPC (also known as a bar code) includes twelve digits, each represented by a unique combination of fat, medium, and thin lines. The first six digits identify the manufacturer. This manufacturer code is what you pay for when you apply for a UPC; you'll use it on every one of your products.

The last six digits identify each product. You make up the first five of these six (using any system you like), and the sixth is a calculated check-digit.

UPCs are born in Dayton, Ohio, in the offices of the Uniform Code Council (UCC). Their cost depends on a company's annual sales volume. It's probably safe to assume that most of the folks reading this book will fall into the "less than $2 million" category, which costs $750 as of this writing (September 2001). That's a one-time cost for coding an unlimited number of products forever.

You can now apply for a UPC on-line or by mail. Check the Web site for information and current details:

www.uc-council.org

Or write:

Uniform Code Council, Inc.
7887 Washington Village Drive, Suite 300
Dayton, OH 45459-8605  USA

Or call:

Phone: 937-435-3870
Fax: 937-435-7317

Your manufacturer code will be sent with several books that tell you waaaay more than you want to know about UPCs. The most relevant information concerns size and position of your bar code. There are different rules for different sorts of packaging. Check the manual for specs on where it should appear on your type of package, what the minimum size is, and the amount of white-space that needs to be left around the symbol.

For a typical sewing/quilting/craft pattern, the UPC should appear in the lower right corner of the back cover, and be about 1½″ wide by 1″ tall, with at least ⅜″ margins on all four sides. If you draw a box 1¾″ high by 2½″ wide, anchored to the right and bottom edges of your pattern back, you should have enough room to insert your UPC art when you get it.

To generate UPC art:

- Use a drawing program that has a bar-code generator built in

- Purchase a stand-alone application

- Hire out the service (it'll probably cost about $20–30 per bar code; check with your printer or with one of the suppliers listed in the books you get with your UPC)

By the way, don't ever say "UPC code" to an editor. We cringe. The "C" already stands for "code."

## Sell Copy

Blaise Pascal said, "This letter is long because I didn't have time to write a short one."

It was tough to be concise in 1656, and it still is today. Even so, you *must* be concise on your cover. Customers cruise the shelves at a fast pace. Once your cover-photo grabs their attention, your sell copy needs to reel them in and convince them to buy.

I include three types of sell copy on my pattern covers:

### Characterizing Phrase

I use a characterizing phrase on my front cover: a few words that summarize the project and explain why the customer needs it.

For instance, for my KinderKakes™ pattern, it's "Perfect as a centerpiece at a baby shower, or simply a unique hand-crafted gift." For my Pocket Scribbler™ pattern, it's "A fun little notekeeper—an exceptional gift!" For Humbug Bag™, the characterizing phrase is "The perfect 'little something' gift—for teachers, grandkids, neighbors, babysitter, etc."

This kind of summary gives customers something to hang their hat on. It entices them to pick the pattern off the rack and investigate further.

### Key Benefits

In my opinion, every cover should include a handful of bullet points that high-light the pattern's most compelling consumer benefits. They tell potential customers at a glance what your pattern will deliver. Key benefits tell customers what they get in exchange for their hard-earned money and convince them that they need your pattern. In other words, key benefits convey that the value consumers receive will be equal or more than the value (price) they pay. And they do all this in three or four short, snappy bullet points.

One of these bullet points may be your characterizing phrase (see above); or the characterizing phrase might be independent.

Your pattern's key benefits might include things like providing creative gratification,

improving skills, and adding flexibility to customer's lives. For instance, on my Jambalaya™ pattern, the bullet points are:

- Use muslin or paper foundations
- Stitch by hand, machine, or both
- Very portable
- Easy, accurate, & fun!

For my Humbug Bag pattern, the cover benefits-list includes:

- The perfect "little something" gift
- Bonus gift tags included
- Easy, fast, & fun!

### Skill Level

Let consumers know whether they've got the skills needed to make your pattern. Can the project be made by a beginner, or does it require advanced skills?

Some designers use a rating system—for instance, a scale of one needle for absolute beginners through five needles for advanced skills. Other designers include this information in a bullet point or burst on the cover; e.g., "Easy Beginner Project!" Others might include it in their descriptive text, e.g., "This project is best suited for the experienced crafter who is looking for a versatile 'canvas' to try a variety of creative techniques."

## Credits

You may want to include credits somewhere on your cover. Particularly if you use a professional editor and/or photographer, crediting them on the cover (1) recognizes their contribution, and (2) conveys the message to potential buyers that you have invested in professional help to make this a top-quality pattern.

## *Full-Color Back Cover?*

The major advantage of a color back cover is the extra room for photos. It allows you to include thumbnails showing alternate color schemes, design variations, etc. Most consumers have difficulty imagining these variations without seeing a picture. If you can show different options, you'll attract more customers.

The major disadvantage of a color back-cover is cost.

You'll have to decide whether the advantages are worth the premium price. Personally, I think a color back-cover gives the pattern a more valuable appearance.

# Chapter 4
# Printing & Packaging

Getting something printed can be intimidating. This chapter will give you an idea of the process, as well as some terms, options, and recommendations for making good decisions about printing and packing your pattern.

## *Format*

### Overall

The most common format for craft, sewing, and quilting patterns is 5½″×8½″, packed into a 2 mil., 6″×9″ zip-lock plastic bag that has a hang-hole centered at top. This format is the most likely to get your pattern accepted by stores, catalogs, and distributors. If you vary from this standard you may encounter resistance based on variations of, "It doesn't fit into my rack." If a retailer can't display your pattern attractively, they can't sell it. Simple as that.

Some pattern designers supply special racks for displaying their patterns, particularly when their format is non-standard. Sometimes this works, other times not. A retailer is unlikely to have extra floor or counter space, so accepting such a display requires them to take something else out. Your pattern line has to be pretty spectacular for that to happen. If it does, however, you end up with an in-store territory that's pretty much your own. If other patterns are not easily displayed on your rack, you have it to yourself. Even so, I don't recommend this approach for a small designer. While the upside is wonderful, the chances of realizing that upside on a large scale are slim. Not to mention the cost of the custom racks. All things considered, I recommend the industry-standard 6″×9″ zip-lock-bag format.

## Covers and Instruction Sheets

Covers are usually either an 8½″×11″ or a 5½″×8½″ sheet. If the former, front and back covers are printed on the same piece of paper (see example on page 33), which is folded in half widthwise. With half-sheet front covers, the back cover can either be printed separately on a 5½″×8½″ sheet or on a panel of the instructions.

Instruction sheets can be any shape or size, as long as they can be cut or folded to fit into the standard 6″×9″ zip-lock bag. If your instructions fit on standard-size copy paper, you can laserprint your own at first, to assess market demand and minimize risk before going to a commercial printer.

Perhaps the closest thing to a "standard" industry format for patterns is a half-sheet color cover (printed on one side) plus a 17″×22″ instruction sheet, printed on one or both sides as necessary. In this format, the back cover is printed on one panel of the instruction sheet; that sheet is then folded three times to finish at 5½″×8½″. Many of the biggies use this because it's cost efficient and consumers are used to it.

A 5½″×8½″ booklet is an attractive alternative format. These are made from 8½″×11″ sheets folded in half and stapled down the middle (called "saddle stitching"). Designer Cheryl Malkowski uses this for her pattern "Too Much Honey." (She also includes a newsprint insert with full-size appliqué patterns; www.quiltwoman.com/b_show_dtl.crm?r=153)

## *Approaches to Printing*

These days, I print at least 5,000 of a new pattern. But I didn't start out printing 5,000.

My first pattern was KinderKakes™ (for making a baby gift out of basics like receiving blankets, pacifiers, etc., assembled to look like a fancy bakery cake). When I came up with the concept, I was working another full-time job. KinderKakes was an idea that I thought might make a great pattern and would be fun to publish. I worked up three attractive and distinctive variations of the design. I did my market research. And I decided it indeed had reasonable market potential.

I had written and produced half a dozen books and hundreds of corporate brochures before that. So I knew how to get a print job ready. Even so, I wasn't *really* sure KinderKakes™ would sell; self-publishing was a brand-new business for me. So I minimized my risk by printing the first batch of patterns in-house. I figured, "If they sell well, then I'll go to a commercial printer for a larger quantity; if they don't, I won't be stuck with a bill for printing and tons of paper that I can't unload."

So I started my pattern publishing venture with the "adhered-photo approach."

## Adhered-Photo Approach

This is a do-it-yourself approach that produces a reasonably professional-looking pattern. It's a good method to get your feet wet in the pattern business. While your cost-per-pattern will be higher than commercial printing, it allows you to print and pay as you go, rather than getting socked with the entire printing bill and a warehouse full of patterns upfront.

The concept is: Print your covers on a laserprinter; then adhere a good-quality color photo-print in the appropriate spot.

Choose a substantial stock for your covers; it doesn't have to be cover-weight, but heavier than regular letter paper will give it a richer feel. Take your photo with you when choosing cover stock. Some photos show off well on textured or colored backgrounds; for others, it's best to choose a plain background and let the photo do the talking.

Note I said "a good-quality color print" above. Even though I took a do-it-yourself approach to printing when I started, I still hired a professional photographer to take the cover shot. The cover is too important to skimp on the image. (See previous chapter.)

Check on quantity discounts for photo reprints. Generally there are several price breaks, e.g., at 25, 50, and 100 copies. The savings can be significant. But realize, too, that you can't make reprints from a single negative forever. Eventually, it will wear out. (1,000 reprints is about the limit.)

Use an ATG gun to adhere photos to covers. This is a pistol-grip dispenser that feeds double-sided stick-um (a 3M/Scotch-brand product; available at art-supply stores). It's cleaner and more efficient than glue-stick, and holds a lot better. Many distributors and retailers are suspicious of glued-on-photo covers, because many designers use cheapo glue-stick and the photos fall off. So attach your photos securely.

If your instructions fit on 8½″×11″ sheets, print them on a laserprinter as you need them. This is how I started. It keeps out-of-pocket expenses and inventory risks as low as possible. Even many specialty papers will feed through a laserprinter with no problems, for instance, newsprint for paper-piecing foundations. (ABC School Supply carries letter-size sheets of newsprint; see Appendix I.) When you start getting regular orders for a hundred or more patterns at a time, it's a more cost-efficient to go to a printer.

If your pattern requires larger than 8½″×11″ sheets, you'll need to go to a printer. For small runs of large sheets, check with a company that does blueprints; sometimes they have better prices than a "normal" commercial printer. And sometimes not.

## Color-Printer Approach

This is similar to the glued-on-photo approach in that you produce covers in your office. Thus it also is a low-risk way to get started—a good way to assess demand before committing to a large commercial print run.

In this approach, you print the entire cover on a color printer. The potential problems with this method include the images sticking to the plastic bag, toner flaking or chipping off, and inks running if the pattern gets wet. None of these makes a good statement about quality. Still, printer technology is improving every day. Experiment with different types of printers and papers to see what gives you the great results you need for your cover photo.

## Commercial Printer Approach

Within the first few weeks of marketing KinderKakes™, I had sold over 1,000 copies. (No, this is not the norm for a new pattern line; I was very lucky with the free "ads" I got with my press releases.) I was absolutely frantic trying to get photo prints, glue them on, print covers and instructions, fold, assemble, pack, and mail. The last straw was the night we had a houseguest, and I got an order from a catalog to ship 400-some patterns the next day. Of course, I only had 24 on hand. Luckily our guest was also a good friend with a great sense of humor, because every warm body in the house was put to work that night.

When you, too, get to this point, the time has come to get covers and instructions printed and folded commercially. To find a good printer, ask friends for referrals; check the Yellow Pages; search the Web for possibilities. See Appendix C for several printers that specialize in patterns for quilting, sewing, needlework, and crafts.

Get three or more estimates for any print job; you'll be astonished at how much they vary. (I've gotten as many as a dozen bids and they've varied by well over 100%.)

Printers tend to specialize in different types of print jobs. Finding one that is best equipped to do the type of job you need is the key to cost-effective printing. It's also the reason you may need to go to two different printers—one for the color cover and another for the black-and-white instructions. Not every printer can do both types of jobs cost-effectively (although many who specialize in one type will farm out the other, so you can do business with just one company).

When getting bids, ask whether it might be cheaper to print your job in a different format than what you're assuming will work best. For instance, it is typically cheaper to print four letter-size pages on one 11″×17″ sheet and fold it twice (to finish at 5½″×8½″), than to print the same four pages on two 8½″×11″ sheets, collate them, and fold once. If you tell the printer what you want, he may assume there's a compelling reason for your format. But if you suggest that your format is flexible, he may be able to help get your costs down without depreciating the final product.

You can often reduce cost without compromising quality by purchasing a thinner paper, particularly if you're printing on only one side (so no problem with bleed-through). Ask to see samples to determine what will work best for your pattern. A thinner paper also reduces weight and thus shipping costs.

### Gang Printing

No, it's not the Crips and the Bloods slaving over a printing press. Gang printing means that multiple jobs are run on the same big press. By running, say, eight 8½″×11″ jobs at once, the printer saves on set-up costs for each. That allows them to charge less than if each was run separately. The down-side is that colors may be compromised. If, say, you're running a country-colors quilt cover and someone else is running a neon-brights sale flyer, the printer has to adjust the press to make both these jobs look their best. Sometimes that means compromising on the color of one for the sake of the others.

If you work with a printer that is ganging jobs, be sure they guarantee your satisfaction: that if the color isn't what you specified, then they will re-do the job until it is right.

### Proofs

The only way to communicate the result you want is to get a color proof (often called a "match print," though it varies by the printing technology) before you go to press. Typically this is an additional step and expense. Be sure to specify when getting bids that you want a color proof. When your job goes on-press, the operator will adjust colors to match your proof. If your finished job doesn't match it, you have grounds to demand that the job be reprinted. Without a proof the operator doesn't know what the colors should be, so you get what you get.

The same advice goes for anything you print: Get a proof before going to print. In these days of digital files, it's almost inevitable that something gets goofed up going from one computer to another. Check and double-check *before* going to press.

If you work with a local printer, you can request to be present for a "press check." That means you want to be there when the first sheets come off the press, to approve the job against the color proof. The advantage of a press check is that you can help the press person adjust final color so that it is to your satisfaction. The disadvantage is that you will have to be "on call" to drop everything and get down to the print floor; it's tough to predict how fast or slow print jobs will run.

## Hybrid Approach

These days, I use a hybrid of the do-it-yourself and commercial-printer approaches. I go right to a commercial printer for my covers, and print a minimum of 5,000 copies. But I print the instruction-sets myself for the first 1,000 or so. That's enough of a sales history to get any feedback I'm likely to get about horrible mistakes in my text or illustrations (so I can fix them before going to a commercial printer). I also gives me a feel for sales potential so I can better estimate print quantity.

## Digital Delivery: PDFs

A relatively new publishing alternative is to let your customers download the pattern from your Web site and print it themselves.

PDF (Adobe's Portable Document Format) is a file type that (theoretically) allows portability between computer platforms while preserving sizes, fonts, graphics, etc. Adobe offers the Reader software (Adobe Acrobat) free, so anyone can read a PDF file. To create a PDF file, however, you need to purchase the writer software (or a program such as PageMaker or InDesign, which includes it).

I say "theoretically" above because personally, I have had a lot of difficulty with PDFs. Many people swear they work perfectly; but they don't for me. Since I don't want to add "computer trouble-shooter" to my job description, I don't offer my patterns as downloadable documents. I figure if I have trouble with PDFs, others will, too.

The big appeal of digital delivery is that you have no printing costs, no warehousing, no shipping, etc. The big risk is that a digital file is easy to pass along; once a customer has it, it can be "shared" very easily. So for now, I file this option under "emerging delivery technology; good potential but kinks to be worked out."

## What Your Commercial Printer Needs

You don't have to work with a local printer. With email and overnight-delivery services, working long-distance barely takes any more time than working with someone in town. Not that there's anything wrong with supporting your local printer (I personally do whenever I can); but you have other options if you need them.

What do you need to give the printer? Ideally, a Zip disk or CD that contains:

- Your finished file (generally a PageMaker or QuarkXpress document, although it might be a PDF or an EPS (Encapsulated PostScript) file; most printers can work with any of these formats)

- All the fonts that you use in the document

- All the graphics—photos and illustrations—that you use in the document

Also provide hard-copy of:

- The pattern, so they know what it's supposed to look like when finished (including folds, showing which panels end up on front and back of the folded piece)

- Complete contact information in case they have questions or problems

- A list of the files on your CD or Zip disk, including version numbers of your software

- Written instructions about what you want, including quantity, printing instructions (e.g., one 11″×17″ sheet, printed both sides, folded twice to finish at 5½″×8½″), type of paper stock, whether you expect to be called for a press check, etc.

Putting all these details in writing is insurance that the job gets done right the first time. Generally you turn everything in to a salesperson, who communicates your needs to the folks who do the prep and printing. Written instructions help to ensure that your message gets through completely and accurately.

If you don't have the equipment or expertise to deliver a print-ready file, most printers can help you pull all your pieces together. Check not only with printers, but with freelance graphic designers if you need assembly help. Temp agencies are springing up that specialize in desktop publishing and computer design. Ask at your community college for recommendations; often students will work relatively cheaply to get the experience. (But be sure they know what they're doing.) And if you need this sort of help, get several estimates.

## How Many to Print?

It depends.

Some patterns will appeal to a large audience; others to a much smaller pool of potential customers. My Humbug Bag™ pattern, for instance, targets the quick-and-easy hand-crafted gift market—a very large market relative to, say, the have-half-a-year-or-more-to-make-a-bed-size-heirloom-quilt market. So you have to understand the size of your potential market, as well as how you plan to promote sales, in order to determine the optimum print quantity.

For a pattern that targets expert appliqué artists and that will be sold strictly by the designer while teaching block-of-the-month classes, that number might be 100. For a pattern with broad appeal that will be marketed aggressively nationally, that number might be 10,000. Depending on price and related sales (e.g., teaching fees, supplies), both of these patterns could be profitable ventures.

Chapter 6 ("Will It Sell?") discusses market size and how to reach your audience.

## *Packaging*

### Plastic Bags

As mentioned, a 6″×9″ (2 mil.) plastic zip-lock bag, with a centered hang-hole at top, is the standard for patterns.

Be sure to buy bags that have vent holes! These allow air to escape once they're sealed, so they can be packed flat and displayed most efficiently. It's an absolute pain to have to hand-punch holes in bags that don't have them (ask me how I know this).

Pattern bags are available pre-opened; in other words, the zip-locks have been released, so you don't have to open them before slipping your pattern pieces inside. Some designers consider this the best thing since sliced bread; others don't see any benefit. You'll have to decide your own preference.

Several reputable bag suppliers are listed Appendix I.

### Assembly

If you have your pattern printed commercially, be sure to let the printer do the folding. That's an inexpensive add-on to the print job, and well worth the extra pennies.

Assembling the pattern is another story. Every quote I've ever gotten from a printer to assemble and pack pattern pieces into bags was outrageously high. So most designers do it in front of the TV, cajole friends and relatives to help, or pay neighborhood kids to do it.

In my experience, 4th- and 5th-graders are the perfect age for this job. I have paid anywhere from 5¢ to 10¢ per pattern over the years, depending on complexity. That has always worked out to more than the minimum wage for all the kids I ever hired. (Well, except for teenagers who are really slow. Especially girls. They're talking, of course. A good reason to pay by the piece rather than by the hour.)

This may be obvious to everyone but me, but you don't have to assemble all the patterns right away. With my first pattern, when I got 10,000 covers and 10,000 sets of instructions back from the printer, for some reason I thought I needed to get them all collated and into bags immediately. It took someone with more common sense than I to point out that this would actually be counterproductive. What if they didn't all sell? Then I'd have to un-assemble them for re-use and/or recycling.

As a rule of thumb, keep enough assembled patterns on hand that you can fill the largest order that could reasonably be anticipated the next day (e.g., if all your distributors placed double their last order on the same day); but more than that is optional.

See Chapter 14, "Filling Orders," for advice on packing, counting, and storing assembled patterns.

# Section II:
# The Marketing Approach

# Chapter 5
# What Is "Marketing"?

Marketing is a great mystery to many people, including designers. But truly, it's mostly common sense—an orientation, seasoned liberally with creative thinking.

The essence of marketing is creating and selling a product from the perspective of delivering *benefits* to your customers. If your intention is to sell your patterns to a mass market, you are more likely to succeed if you adopt a marketing approach right from the start.

Marketing is more than advertising and promotion. It includes all the things that contribute to convincing a consumer to buy your product: the image/promise of the package, the venue in which it is offered for sale, the position on the shelf (or the catalog page), the advertising you place, the promotional offer(s) you make, the price you set. It's a complicated equation, to be sure. And there's more than one way to make all the elements add up. But that's a big part of what makes marketing so much fun!

One excellent Web site for marketing information is sponsored by the SBA (Small Business Association): www.onlinewbc.org/docs/market/

## The Marketing Mix

Marketing gurus often break the process into five components (or sometimes four or six, depending on how they're defined), which together are called "the marketing mix." These components are:

- Product
- Package
- Price
- Distribution
- Advertising/Publicity/Promotion

These five work together to help make a sale. These topics are covered in detail in separate chapters, but let's begin with an overview to put them into perspective:

## Product

The essential starting point to effective marketing is understanding precisely what you're selling—your "product"—and who you're selling it to—your "target audience." Your product is not "a pattern"; it's typically something like "fun," "surprising and delighting my grandchild," "an impressive home decoration," etc. Your product is the need being filled—the benefits that convince the consumer to exchange hard-earned dollars for your instructions.

Chapter 6, "Will It Sell?" addresses the topics of product and audience.

## Package

Your "package" includes everything the consumer sees—words, pictures, graphics, colors, etc.—as well as the physical characteristics that affect handling of your product through the distribution system.

Package is covered in Chapters 2, 3, and 4, "Writing Instructions," "The Cover," and "Printing & Packaging," respectively.

## Price

The essence of proper pricing is that the consumer believes your product will deliver equal or greater value (*benefits*) than that of the dollars they exchange for it. When that situation exists, a sale occurs.

See Chapter 7, "Pricing," for details.

## Distribution

"Distribution" is how you get your patterns to end-customers. That might be direct-to-consumer sales at shows; it might be through the mail, in response to magazine ads; it might be by wholesaling your patterns to shop owners, who in turn, re-sell them to consumers. Any or all of these—as well as other distribution channels such as distributors and catalogs and the Web—may be part of your marketing plan. The ones you pursue will depend on your target market: What's the most efficient and effective way to reach potential customers?

Chapter 8, "Distribution," talks about these venues and how to succeed in each.

## Advertising, Publicity & Promotion

Advertising builds awareness and establishes a distinctive image for your product and company. Publicity, in simplistic terms, is free advertising. Promotion encourages a sale *now*.

Whereas advertising and publicity build image and awareness of your products over the long run ("That looks good; I might buy it someday"), promotion provides an incentive for increasing short-term volume ("I'll take one today"). As a rule, advertising effectiveness can only be measured over the long term; and promotional offers have a short deadline as an incentive for immediate action.

Chapters 9, 10, and 11 cover these three important topics.

## *Tracking & Analysis*

Finally, a marketing approach means learning from what you do and adjusting as necessary to improve in the future. Chapter 12 gives tips for effective tracking and analysis.

## Chapter 6
# Will It Sell?

You've got a great design. Your family and friends love it. But can you make a profit selling it as a pattern?

There is no crystal ball or magic formula that will tell you for sure. Nobody—including huge companies like Ford (remember the Edsel?), Colgate (what was the name of that black toothpaste?), and Coca Cola (the "new" Coke?)—knows how consumers are going to react to a new product. But you do the research and play the odds. Yes, it's a risk; but it's a calculated risk. And seven or eight times out of ten it'll be profitable; and once or twice out of ten it'll be tremendously profitable; and, well, let's not think about the remaining two or three times. The point is, you can determine whether the odds are in your favor by doing some basic market research and analysis.

### What Are You Selling?

First of all, what exactly are you selling? The surface answer is "a pattern." But to assess whether it's going to be a winner in the marketplace, you need to delve a bit deeper. Just as Tide is not selling laundry detergent but rather clean clothes, you are not selling a pattern but the promise of something: a finished quilt (or vest or doll or whatever), a fun experience, a hand-made gift that will impress and bring joy to the recipient, etc.

This promise—the customer *benefit*—is the reason that customers buy your pattern.

## Who Is Your Market?

Now that you know what you are selling, think about the type of person who is most likely to want that/those benefit(s). For instance, if your pattern is intricate or complicated, it will appeal to consumers with the time and skill necessary to complete it rather than beginners or the quick-and-easy crowd. If it's a baby gift, it will appeal to people who are expecting a new baby in their lives.

Describe a typical customer in terms of demographics (i.e., things like age, sex, income) and psychographics (i.e., things like values, attitudes, and aspirations). This is your "target market." Be as detailed as you can, but also remain flexible. Once you start selling a pattern, you may be surprised at some of the people who can't live without your products.

If profit is one of your aims, then next assess whether your market is big enough to be profitable. "Big" can be either in people or dollars. There are more beginner than expert sew-ers, quilters, crafters, dollmakers, etc. So in terms of number of people who might potentially be interested, a pattern that appeals to beginners will have the larger market potential. But while fewer in number, experts tend to be heavy spenders in pursuing their passion. So a pattern that appeals to experts might find a bigger market in terms of dollars, even though the absolute number of customers is smaller.

How do you get a handle on these numbers? Research!

Trade organizations and magazines often conduct surveys to help manufacturers and retailers understand and expand the market. Results of these studies are widely published in trade magazines and on Web sites, and generally get at least summary coverage in consumer magazines and newspapers. Appendix E lists some prominent trade publications and organizations. Chances are you already subscribe to the major consumer magazines in your field. Others can be identified at the library (particularly guild libraries), by searching the Web, or from reference books such as the annual *Writer's Market* (see Appendix J).

For instance, a few pertinent statistics that have been published recently, based on year 2000 data:

- According to CODA (the Craft Organization Directors Association), crafts are a $13 billion industry in the United States.
- According to HIA (the Hobby Industry Association), crafts and hobbies are a $23 billion industry. Of that total, general crafts accounted for 41% ($9 billion), needlecrafts accounted 34% ($8 billion), painting & fishing (don't ask me who decided to lump those two categories together!) for 16% ($4 billion), and floral for 9% ($2 billion).
- According to the Quilting in America 2000 survey (commissioned jointly by *Quilter's Newsletter Magazine* and International Quilt Market & Festival), quilting is a $1.8 billion industry in the United States, with almost 20 million quilters. Of those, just over 1 million are "dedicated" quilters, spending over $500 annually and accounting for 94% of quilt-industry expenditures.
- According to the HSA (Home Sewing Association), there are 31 million "current sew-ers" (defined as women who sew more than putting on a button). They spent over $3 billion last year, and fully 50% of those who sew are between the ages of 35 and 54 (hardly the "little old lady" stereotype!).

You can also assess the viability of your concept by looking around and talking to people. Look at catalogs and talk to shop owners to see what's selling. Ask some of the type of people you hope will buy your pattern what they think of your idea (e.g., consumers, shop owners, catalog buyers, guild or club members); most folks are delighted to be asked and to give their opinion. If you teach, your students—and how fast your classes fill—will give you valuable feedback on market potential. Listen on the Internet (for instance, on email lists and newsgroups specific to your product type) to hear what people are making, what they want to make, what kinds of things they have trouble with, techniques they'd like to learn, etc., to determine genuine consumer wants and needs.

## How Will You Reach Them?

Okay. You know what you're selling and you know who is likely to buy it. Next, can you reach them affordably?

The old aphorism, "If you build a better mousetrap, people will beat a path to your door," only works if the path is clearly marked. These days, there are so many things vying for consumers' attention that it takes a focused effort to break through. How might you let your target market know you have a product that they want? What will it cost to reach them?

Is there a magazine or newsletter whose readership shares the same demographics as your target, in which you could advertise and/or promote your pattern? Is there a certain type of store that carries patterns like yours, or a dedicated department within a larger store? Are there trade and/or consumer shows that attract exactly the folks you are looking for? Is there a distributor that specializes in your type of pattern? Does your target consumer search the Web for products like yours? (As of 2001, 70% of people who sew use the Internet.) And what are the most promising of these vehicles likely to cost?

The point, of course, is that you have to be able to reach your audience affordably. If it costs you $2 to tell each customer about your product and you only have $1 built into the pricing structure for this, the money truck will be making a pick-up rather than a delivery.

## Why Should They Buy Yours?

You've determined that there is an adequate audience for your product, and that you can reach them affordably. The final question to answer is: What is the compelling reason for them to buy *your* pattern over all the other products competing for their dollars? In marketing parlance, this is your *unique selling proposition*, or your *point of difference* versus the competition. It's what makes your pattern stand out from the crowd. It's the crucial factor in winning the sale versus a competitor.

Your point(s) of difference can be just about anything. It can be a prestigious name; Rolex uses this to win sales versus Timex. It might be price; generic cat food versus the name-brand. In my opinion, the best unique selling proposition is based on exceptional quality plus excellent value.

Exceptional quality is self-explanatory. Value is a little more complicated.

Value is not the same as price. An excellent value is when the customer feels they are getting more than they paid. Whether they paid a lot or just a few dollars, what they received was worth it and then some. Value is often judged in comparison to similar products. Consumers understand the market, know what they typically get for a certain price, know what a typical pattern is like. So if you can give them a pattern that is of recognizably higher quality than the norm for the same price, they will feel that they've gotten great value. And that's a very good feeling to cultivate among your customers.

To figure out your unique selling proposition, list everything that makes your pattern different from, and better than, the competition. (This implies that you know your competition intimately. If you don't, find out!) Sort through your list to figure out which of them are most likely to convince your target customer to buy. Which one(s) will shift the balance in favor of your product when prospects are weighing their purchase decision?

If you don't have a compelling point of difference—at least one thing that is significantly better about your product than any other—you don't have a strong product concept. It may sell, but the odds for building a profitable business on it are not in your favor.

# What Makes a Pattern a Commercial Success?

*by Ann Anderson, distributor and publisher, QuiltWoman.com*

I don't pretend to have the definitive answer to this question. But as a distributor, I do track the performance of and hear feedback about *lots* of patterns; and from this experience, I've drawn a few of conclusions.

My best-selling patterns all have one thing in common: They offer a great value to everyone in the distribution chain—distributors, retailers, and consumers. Humbug Bag™ from Make It Easy Sewing & Crafts® is a good example. (www.make-it-easy.com)

Among the values it delivers to consumers:

- Pattern can be used many times, and each bag personalized to fit the recipient—so it's not a one-shot deal.
- Bag can be made in half-an-hour or less—instant gratification.
- The instructions are clear and easy enough for beginners. Yet the project lends itself to design variations and trying new techniques (it's basically a "blank canvas" for creativity) so it also appeals to those with advanced and adventuresome skills, too.
- The instructions include several extras beyond the project instructions, such as machine-quilting lessons and gift tags. Consumers feel like they're getting more than they paid for.

Humbug Bag delivers excellent values to retailers, too:

- Pattern can be used to teach a variety of techniques and to attract a variety of audiences to their store, from kids' learn-to-sew classes to holiday clubs.
- Pattern can be used to sell other stuff, from supplies (e.g., complete kits) to sewing machines (as demo projects).

And finally, distributors get a major benefit:

- A pattern that sells in large volume, as consumers and retailers pull it through the distribution chain.

I've also noticed that patterns that incorporate a new and/or interesting technique generally have a better chance of selling well. Stack-and-whack, watercolor quilts, and faux chenille are current well-known examples. Mexican Stars and other patterns from Annette Ornelas/Southwind Designs include an ingenious and fun technique for making curves; they are selling very well. (www.southwindquilts.com) Retailers, teachers, and consumers are always interested in fun new techniques.

I think a catchy name is also a big asset. Humbug Bag, for instance, and Stack-n-Whack come to mind. A little wallhanging entitled Nun of the Above, designed by Jeannie Aschenbrenner of Garden Gate Press, sold well for me at Quilt Market, and I think the fun name had a lot to do with it. (www.quiltwoman.com/b_show_dtl.cfm?r=382)

While there's no magic formula for success in the pattern business, history does at least offer a few clues.

# Chapter 7

# Pricing

Okay, I'll confess right here at the outset: I don't have any training in accounting (my business training is in marketing). Still, I do know one thing about accounting: You have to take in more than you pay out if you want to make a profit. And that's the foundation for all my pricing calculations. So if my system seems naïve or even ridiculous to those of you more educated in this area than I, please forgive me and recognize that, despite its faults, this system has worked well for me in building a profitable pattern business.

That said, pricing is one of the thorniest issues you have to deal with as a publisher. So much is based on assumptions; and you know what they say about "assume." Still, you need a price. And you want to establish one that will work for you for several years. (This is particularly important if you work with distributors and/or catalogs, since price changes involve substantial time and expense for them, from reprinting price lists to updating their ordering and payment systems.)

As a business person, you need to figure out at what price you make the optimum profit. A lower-priced item will almost always sell more units than a higher-priced item. It's simply more affordable to more people. However, it is also possible that your profit will be greater by charging a high price on a low volume. For instance, selling 10 items at $10 profit each nets $100; selling 100 items at 80¢ profit each nets $80. So price and profit are kind of a balancing act: What is the likely volume at different price points, and which of them gives you the largest profit?

There are whole books written on pricing. (One good one is by Sylvia Landman, called *Pricing Guidelines for Arts & Crafts : Successful, Professional Crafters Share Their Pricing Strategies to Help You Set Profitable Prices for Your Art*; see Appendix J). The system I use follows, and as stated, is intuitive rather than by-the-books. So consider it simply an introduction to a big, complex topic and check other resources, too.

## General Approach

How much to charge? Big, big question. Too much, and nobody will buy it. Too little, and you won't make enough profit to stay in business. Personally, I look at price from two perspectives:

- How much money I need to make to cover my costs and earn a reasonable profit
- Market "comps," i.e., what comparable patterns are selling for.

Then I compare the two. If one is substantially different from the other, it's back to the drawing board to figure out how to bring the two more in line.

## Costs

If you can't more-than-cover your costs, you'll lose money. That's common sense. So the first thing to figure is what it costs to make and market a pattern.

Note: If your goal is mass-market sales, I recommend that you figure costs based on large-volume rather than test-market quantities. That way, you'll know what to price at if you're successful. Although you'll make a little less on your start-up patterns (due to higher per-pattern costs for small quantities), you won't have to change your price as you grow.

What are your costs? They fall into three general catatories:

### Per-Design Costs

These are expenses that are the same whether you sell one or 100,000 patterns of a single design:

- Concept development (materials and labor)
- Photography and digitizing
- Production (writing, graphics, layout, etc.)
- Advertising/promotion/publicity
- Legal (advice, registrations, etc.)

### Per-Pattern Costs

This type of expense varies depending on the number of patterns of a particular design you print and sell:

- Printing (covers and instructions)
- Packaging (materials and assembly)
- Delivery (envelopes and boxes, postage)

### Overhead Costs

These are your costs of doing business. They apply to all your patterns, not just one design. These tend to grow incrementally, as your business expands to each next level:

- Equipment (computer, programs, etc.)
- Space/utilities (rent, telephone, etc.)
- Accounting/bookkeeping/taxes
- Registration fees (business license, UPC, etc.)
- Legal (consulting, general business issues)
- Advertising/promotion/publicity (e.g., trade shows)
- Employees (someday!)

## Profit

If one of your goals is to make a profit, then you need to take that into consideration when determining price. (Profit is above and beyond getting reimbursed for expenses and paid for your labor.) How much profit do you need for publishing your own patterns to be worth your time and energy?

This is a judgement call, within reason. If you figure too high a profit into your pricing

## Costs: An example

The following figures are in the ballpark for printing 5,000 copies of a pattern. Your mileage may vary, depending on the particulars of your design.

*Per-design costs:*

- Concept/samples                   $500
- Photography                         300
- Labor (writing, layout, etc.)   2,000
- Advertising/promotion           2,000
- Legal/registration fees            200
  Subtotal                         $5,000

*Per-pattern costs:*

- Printing/cutting/folding
  Color covers                     $400
  Instruction sets                  800
- Plastic bags                      150
- Assembly                          500
- Mailing envelopes/boxes           150
  Subtotal                       $2,000

*Overhead costs:*

These vary considerably based on what you include. If you want a UPC, for instance, that's $750 (one-time cost). If you go to a trade show every year, that's several thousand dollars.

Subtotal                          $2,000

Total costs to produce this hypothetical pattern are thus $9,000 ($1.80 per pattern).

Profit at, say, $.80 per pattern adds another $4,000, for a total of $13,000 ($2.60 per pattern).

(Don't panic! These are not all out-of-pocket expenses. And while 5,000 patterns is a reasonable number for mass-market profitability, you don't have to start there.)

calculation, you may overprice the product and reduce sales. For a $10 (retail) pattern, I think a profit of $.50 to $1 per pattern is reasonable.

## Putting It All Together

Total costs plus a reasonable profit for a hypothetical pattern are $13,000 for 5,000 patterns (see example at left). Of that total, only $3,700 are out-of-pocket expenses (i.e., you need to write a check for them):

*Per-design costs:*
- Concept/samples (assumes
      $300 is your labor)          $200
- Photography                       300
- Advertising/promotion (assumes
      $1,000 is your labor)       1,000
- Legal/registration fees           200
  Subtotal                       $1,700

*Per-pattern costs:*
- Printing/cutting/folding
  Color covers                     $400
  Instruction sets                  800
- Plastic bags                      150
- Assembly                          500
- Mailing envelopes/boxes           150
  Subtotal                       $2,000

The remaining $9,300 are for your labor, overhead, and profit. They're not out-of-pocket costs (assuming that you do the writing, design, layout, and publicity yourself). And while you certainly want to get paid for your work, you don't actually have to take money out of the bank to pay yourself immediately.

I find it useful to determine the number of patterns I need to sell in order to cover my out-of-pocket expenses, i.e., to know where the dividing line is between losing real dollars and not. In our example, I have to write checks for $3,700 to get my design published. If I get an average of $8 each for them, once I've sold 463 patterns ($3,700 ÷ $8), then I'm on the payroll.

Can I sell that many? If not, can I reduce my costs? Or raise my price? Or a combination of both? Work the numbers until you come up with a price and quantity that you're confident is do-able.

Obviously, if building a pattern business is your goal, then simply covering out-of-pocket costs is *not* the aim; you want to get paid for your time as well as make a profit. Still, it's a good perspective to figure as a worst-case scenario in building your business plan.

## Adjusting for Distributor/ Wholesale Sales

Most people know that products are typically sold to retail accounts at half their suggested retail price (SRP). In other words, a pattern that sells to consumers for $8 costs the shop (wholesaler) $4.

Many people don't know that distributors (and also most catalogs and mail-order businesses) demand an additional 30% discount off that 50% wholesale price (which works out to a total of 65% off the retail price). The designer gets 35% of the suggested retail price for distributor sales. Thus, if you need to get $2.60 per pattern in order to cover expenses and make a profit, your retail price has to be $7.50 ($2.60 ÷ 35%). (See page 61 for why it's worth paying this percentage.)

You will likely sell some patterns at full retail; others at wholesale; and still others at distributor prices. The proportion of each is likely change over time, shifting from mostly direct-to-consumer to mostly distributor sales. I recommend figuring price based on selling 100% to distributors. Consider the little extra you make at the start from wholesale and retail sales as wiggle room.

## Market Comps

The other angle from which I approach pricing is what realtors call "comps." What are comparable patterns selling for? The question to answer is: What are customers likely to be willing to pay for a pattern such as yours?

If you are not concerned with making a profit, this may be the only analysis you need in order to determine a selling price. Simply pick a price that is in line with what customers expect to pay for comparable patterns.

If your goal is mass-market sales and a profit, however, you need to compare results from the two approaches. Let's look at the three possible scenarios for comps. Assume that you've figured you need to sell your pattern at $10 retail to cover costs and make a profit.

### Yours Is More Expensive

If patterns similar to yours are selling for $5 and you're asking $10, consumers will probably feel that your pattern is overpriced. The exception is if you have an incredibly compelling benefit over those other patterns, and the ability/means to convey that message to consumers.

### Yours Is Close

If patterns similar to yours are selling for $9, that's close enough to negotiate with yourself. Can you be happy with a little less profit? Or can you be more aggressive in marketing them so you bump up total sales? Do you have (or can you add) a benefit versus the others that justifies a slight premium in price? Or a little bit of each?

### Yours Is Less Expensive

If patterns similar to yours are selling for $20, first ask yourself if you're overlooking a significant expense (for instance, if competitors mainly sell at consumer shows, they have to include the cost of booth rentals and travel into their cost of doing business; do you?). If not, you've got a tiger by the tail!

## Whole-Dollar vs. $.95 Pricing

There is a proven psychological advantage to pricing using the $.95 or $.99 system for commodity products. People feel that they're paying less, even though they know better in the logical part of their brain.

Personally, I don't think it matters with original-design patterns. I recommend pricing patterns using a whole-dollar amount. It will certainly make bookkeeping easier.

# Chapter 8
# Distribution

Distribution is how you get your patterns to end-customers. The three broad distribution methods are:

- Selling directly to consumers
- Selling to retailers, who then sell to consumers
- Selling to distributors, who then sell to retailers who then sell to consumers

Each of these has its advantages and disadvantages:

With direct-to-consumer (i.e., retail) sales, you get paid more money per pattern (full retail price). You also have a personal relationship with your customers. But it takes a lot of time to sell patterns one by one. You're only one person with 24 hours a day (you don't need to sleep, right?), which limits the potential number of customers you can reach directly.

With both retailer and distributor (i.e., wholesale) sales, the big advantage is the multiplier effect: Instead of just one person (you) selling your patterns, you now have help—experienced help, with contacts, connections, and budgets of their own. Retailers and distributors will promote your patterns to their customers at their own expense. That saves you time and money—resources that you can then spend designing and printing more patterns.

The main perceived disadvantage of selling wholesale is that you get less money per pattern. Retailers pay you 50% of your suggested retail price (SRP); and distributors pay 35% of SRP (see page 54). However, once volume is taken into account, you will likely end up with more money in your pocket by selling to wholesalers than direct to consumers. I certainly did.

Let's look at some of the ways you can get your patterns to consumers, retailers, and distributors, respectively.

## Selling Directly to Consumers

Selling directly to consumers (i.e., selling retail) is where most designers start. If your goal in self-publishing is one-on-one sales (teachers, for instance), this is where you'll park your car. Patterns that don't clearly fit into a standard category, and patterns that don't promote sales of other items in a shop are also likely to remain direct-to-consumer "niche" items.

For instance, my KinderKakes™ and BridalBakes™ patterns (for making "cakes" out of baby and bridal gifts) sell mainly direct-to-consumer. They don't fit neatly into any existing category in most stores. They're not dolls or bags or quilts; they don't necessarily sell fabric or notions; they're not towels or receiving blankets, even though they're made with them. They simply don't fit into a standard category. Which is why my proportion of sales of these two patterns is skewed toward individual consumers and specialty catalogs, versus my clearly categorizable patterns, which sell 90% to wholesalers and 10% to consumers.

If your goal is to reach a mass market, however, selling retail is generally a means to an end. It's where you start in order to establish a track record that will you help convince wholesalers to carry your line.

There are many ways to sell directly to consumers. If you teach, you can sell patterns directly to your students. (If you teach on behalf of a shop or organization—e.g., a retail store, guild, on-line store, community college, etc.—

be sure to work out with the owner/manager whether you can sell directly to students or if the organization wants to carry the patterns). Some other popular retail venues are:

### Direct Mail

Okay, let's be blunt. Most folks consider direct mail "junk mail" (postal service) or "spam" (email). Your challenge is to avoid being thought of in either of those terms.

With direct mail, you send your offer to individual consumers via the post office, a delivery service, or email. The success of a direct-mail campaign depends on the quality of the list you're mailing to. Let's say you have two lists. One includes only people who fit your target market very closely, and the other is a random selection of folks from the phone book. Which list is going to be more effective at selling your patterns? Understand the quality of your list before licking that first stamp!

Some ways to get lists: compile your own (e.g., past customers); trade with other designers; or buy one. Many magazines sell their mailing lists for one-time direct-mail use. Or you can hire a list broker to create a custom list that meets your demographic specifications. To find a list broker, check the Yellow Pages, ask the advertising manager of a magazine for a recommendation, or check at the library in directories such as *Direct Marketing List Sources*. The quality of brokered lists varies tremendously. Some brokers are great, others not so great. Check references.

As a rule of thumb, your item needs to sell for $20 or more for a postal direct-mail campaign to be cost-effective. Email, of course, is far less expensive. Response rates vary but for estimating, you can figure that less than 5% of a good list will purchase (often closer to 1%).

### Consumer Shows

From local guild shows to giant national expos, there are many opportunities to sell your patterns at consumer extravaganzas. And the pay-off can be much more than simply selling your patterns: for instance networking, customer-relationship-building, leads for other gigs (teaching, lectures), and gathering market intelligence.

Costs to exhibit vary by venue, but typically you will have to cover a booth-rental fee, plus travel and lodging, plus shipping (to and from), plus your display costs. For a big national show, these expenses can easily run $4,000 and more. So you need to sell a lot of patterns, or pick up several related gigs (e.g., teaching, lectures), for that to be profitable as your primary distribution system.

One way to boost sales at shows is to teach classes (or do demos, trunk shows, etc.) that showcase your projects and/or techniques. Your enthusiasm will infect your audience, and they'll rush back to your booth after class to buy your patterns. If you do this, be sure that the class isn't just an infomercial. That won't endear you to customers. Give them something substantive that relates to your patterns.

Even if you can't entirely cover your costs for consumer shows from pattern sales, it might be worth making up the difference from your advertising/publicity/promotion budget. Your presence at such shows tells consumers you exist, that you're professional, and it makes them aware of the sorts of products you have for sale. Though they may not buy at the show, the fact that you've built awareness and credibility may pave the way for a future sale.

To find out about shows, check the ads in magazines and newsletters, ask friends, and search the Web. Get on a few mailing lists, and eventually the shows will find you. Some of the bigger shows are listed in Appendix F.

### Being There Without Being There

You can also participate in consumer shows without having a booth of your own. I often consign patterns and lend models to one or more selected retailers at consumer shows. Pick a retailer that you trust and that you know will do a good job featuring your pattern(s). Even better, give them enough lead time to develop a class or demo around your pattern.

## Bricks and/or Clicks Stores

"Bricks" are physical storefronts; "clicks" are virtual store, i.e., on the Web. If you have a store of either type, by all means sell your patterns directly to consumers there, even if it's not your primary distribution venue.

Most small publishers will not have a physical store; but I believe all should have a presence on the Web. You don't have to have your own site; you can sell your patterns to Web-based shops who will feature and sell your patterns on-line (see "Selling to Retailers" later in this chapter). But there are many advantages to having your own site.

### Why Your Own Web Site?

A Web site is both a distribution method and an advertising/publicity/promotion tool.

As an advertising/publicity/promotion tool, having your own Web site says, "I'm real." It lends you professional credibility. It helps people to find your products. Many, many consumers gather information for making purchase decisions by searching that vast virtual resource-center called the Internet. And their number is increasing every day. The latest figure I read is that 70% of those who quilt, sew, and/or craft use the Web.

As a distribution method, having a Web storefront gives your customers a place to buy if they can't find your patterns locally. But recognize that a Web site is essentially passive: It requires customers to come to you. Simply existing in cyberspace is not enough. You have to advertise and promote it, to entice them to visit. I could always correlate spikes in Web sales with "active" efforts (such as a space ad or a promotional offer) that I delivered directly to my target audience.

My own experience is that Web sales increase naturally over time, as your reputation grows; but they'll probably only ever be 10% of your total sales; distributors and wholesale accounts will be the other 90%.

## Building a Web Site

There are many books and Web-based resources about building and maintaining a Web site. This section only scratches the surface, to get you pointed in the right directions.

Spend the money to get your own domain name (URL). Free sites sound appealing, but in the long run you'll regret it. They often put your entire site in a "frame" (exactly what it sounds like: a fence around your pages) that causes many search engines to bypass your content (they're programmed to ignore everything inside a frame). So nobody can find you, which defeats the purpose of having a Web site in the first place. Owning your name also makes it easier to move your site if you need to.

Your choice of a Web host is important, too. Choose one that you are confident will be in business for a long time, and one that provides great customer service. One of many services that rates and compares hosts is http://hottesthosts.com. Search for "Web hosts" to find other rating services.

You don't need to learn how to write HTML code (the language of the Net; HyperText Markup Language) to have a Web site. You can, of course; and many designers do (see sidebar by Patti Anderson). But if that's not your thing, you can hire someone to do it for you.

Even if you hire someone to build your site, you'll still have to tell them what you want on the pages, i.e., write and design it. Don't just jump in and write/design as you would a print piece. Instead, start with some research about how Web search engines work. That will help you to craft your page titles, META-tags, keywords, copy, and design so your site is most likely to be found. You can find lots of current information on these topics on the Web. A few good sites to get you started:

- www.ReallyBig.com
- www.BigNoseBird.com
- www.WebPagesThatSuck.com
- "Getting Listed by the Major Search Engines," www.geocities.com/SiliconValley/Campus/1282/

For instance, when writing/designing a Web page, use words rather than graphics at the top of your pages. Choose words that customers are likely to use in search requests. Search engines typically look at the highest (physically) item on a page to see if it matches

---

### Learning to Speak "Web"

*by Patti R. Anderson, designer, teacher, and quiltmaker, Patchpieces*

When I decided to create a Web site I knew nothing about HTML. My goal was to create an educational Web site, as well as a place to sell my patterns. In the Spring of 1999, with the help of friends, my teenage daughters, and a great book, I jumped in full speed ahead. And in less than a month, Patchpieces.com was launched.

The book I used was *Creating Web Pages Simplified* by MaranGraphics. It led me step-by-step through the entire process, from organizing pages to uploading files. I found the book's illustrations particularly helpful because they're graphics from Netscape Composer (a free Web-page editor included with Netscape Communicator), which I already owned, and it was free!

What I like best about Composer is that it translates into HTML for you. You create a page exactly like it will look on the Internet. As you work, Composer is humming along in the background, converting your text and graphics to HTML and saving it all in a nice, neat package.

Since those early days, I have learned a great deal of HTML in order to fix problems, insert tags for on-line shopping, and similar tweaks. I have also bought lots of software to help manipulate and optimize my graphics. However, I am still using Composer, and it's serving me well.

And you know what? Now I'm using my new skills to create Web pages for on-line courses I teach at QuiltUniversity.com!

the search criteria. They can't read photos and graphics, so if that's what's highest on your page, your site may be ignored.

### Selling Via Collectives

Collectives are a relatively new kind of Web site: many individual sites under one umbrella (kind of a virtual merchant mall). You pay to camp under their umbrella, but they take care of building and maintaining your site, and they advertise and promote to bring customers to the umbrella site. An example:

- Quilter's Warehouse (collective); www.quilterswarehouse.com

## Selling to Retailers

Rather than selling one pattern to one consumer, you can sell a dozen patterns to one retailer (wholesale), and let the retailer find twelve consumers to buy them. This saves you time by reducing the number of packages you have to send; and it increases your exposure by getting your pattern in front of more potential customers than you could contact on your own. Of course, you have to pay for this.

### Wholesale Price Formula

Retailers typically expect a 50% discount from the suggested retail price for patterns.

### Identifying Prospects

How do you get in touch with retailers to make your pitch? First you must identify them.

### Bricks-and-Mortar Retailers

You can compile your own list of retailers from numerous sources. Many stores have Web sites (these often give you a feel for the type of merchandise the shop sells; no sense trying to sell a traditional quilt pattern to a shop that focuses on contemporary, or a vest pattern to a shop that specializes in dolls). Many are included at www.quiltindex.com.

You can compile names and addresses from phone books (your library has copies for other cities), directories (e.g., programs from consumer and trade shows, directories published by trade organizations), and magazine ads.

Travel guides are another possibility. Many localities and organizations publish guides to specific types of shops and artisans. The book *Quilter's Traveling Companion* (see Appendix J) is an outstanding example of this type of resource.

You might also invite retailers to send you their contact information. For instance, QuiltWoman.com offers a registry service for shops (www.quiltwoman.com/shop_add.cfm). When a shop registers, it's added to a searchable database, which consumers can use to find the shops (by type or location) they're looking for (www.quiltwoman.com/shop_fnd.cfm). This provides a valuable service to both shops and consumers, and gives QuiltWoman.com an up-to-date list of prospects. Everyone benefits.

Another way to identify potential customers is to go where there are lots of them in one place at one time: in other words, a trade show. Appendix F lists several big ones. While mounting a booth at these venues is expensive (often several thousand dollars), it makes finding your target audience very easy. Store owners are there specifically to consider products like yours. (More on doing trade shows later in this chapter and in Chapter 10.)

### Mail-Order Catalogs

Catalogs buy and re-sell your patterns, the same as a bricks-and-mortar store would, except they are often both retailers and wholesalers. As such, they will request/demand distributor pricing. Sometimes the percentage discount is negotiable.

Personally, I recommend that if they buy in sufficient quantity to meet your minimums, give them the distributor price. You'll make it up in volume, goodwill, and exposure.

There are lots of catalogs, as anyone with a mailbox knows. Search the Web, get on a few mailing lists, ask other designers, etc. Appendix H lists a few places to start.

### Virtual Stores

Don't overlook Web retailers (virtual storefronts). Mail-order catalogs often have a virtual storefront in addition to their paper catalog. Often, it's easier to get accepted by these sorts of retailers than either distributors or bricks-and-mortar operations because their overhead is lower. Some may work on a consignment basis, however. A few examples:

- QuiltWoman.com (distributor & Web retailer); www.quiltwoman.com
- Patterncrafts (mail-order catalog & Web retailer); www.patterncrafts.com
- Pattern Showcase (Web retailer); www.patternshowcase.com
- Pieceful Acre Patterns (Web retailer); www.piecefulacrepatterns.com

### Selling to Chains

I've only dipped my toes into this class of trade (at WalMart, Target, and Jo-Ann ETC), but my conclusion is that these types of retailers are beyond the resources of most small publishers. They use very sophisticated just-in-time ordering systems (that require a special computer program and link), and they literally have a book's worth of rules and regulations about how to order, how to ship, how to invoice, etc. You need a staff to comply with all their rules.

I don't mean to discourage you. If you have a pattern that you believe would sell well in a chain, it may be worthwhile to invest in the equipment and other resources required to work with them. They certainly can push big volume! I'm just warning you that there's far more involved—time, investment, resources—in working with this class of trade than others.

It is possible for a small publisher/ designer to get into stores like Target and WalMart on a local basis. You need to convince the manager (or special-events coordinator) that your presence and product will benefit to the store. Generally that means increasing sales of other items in the store, not just making a profit on your patterns.

You are most likely to get in this way for special events. For instance, I was able to get into my local Target for a day with my KinderKakes™ pattern for their annual baby-fair event. And into WalMart for a weekend because the local manager liked my stuff, and was willing to consider it because my husband used to lifeguard for her father 30 years ago (you never know what contacts will work out!).

Still, for a small publisher, it's probably best to let a distributor handle orders to the big chains for you.

## The Approach

While vending at a trade show is probably the most efficient and effective way to approach retailers, you can sell to them via letter/phone.

If you're going the letter/phone route, address your pitch to the person who makes the buying decisions. Call to ask who this is— and be sure to confirm spelling. By calling to confirm name and address, you give the shop an opportunity to ask you to make your pitch by phone if they want, or to receive it by mail if they're not in a position to consider it when you call.

If you call on shops in person, make an appointment (with the buyer, of course). By conveying a professional image right from the start, you'll instill confidence that you will conduct your business in an equally professional manner—which often is an important factor in a buyer's decision.

Assuming you haven't been invited to sell your product over the phone, write a short (one page at most) letter addressed to the buyer describing the appeal of your pattern, how you believe it will boost their shop sales, and basic terms of purchase (i.e., wholesale price, suggested retail price, minimum purchase quantity, whether they or you pay postage, when payment is due, etc.). If possible, include a pattern cover or sell sheet so they can grasp what you're selling at a glance. (A sell sheet includes a picture of your product and a headline plus bullet points that highlight customer benefits.)

Make it easy for the buyer to request a free sample pattern if they're enticed by your introductory letter. Many shop owners want to test a new pattern before offering it for sale, to be sure the quality is up to their standards. In my opinion, they shouldn't have to pay for a pattern they're auditioning.

When you receive a request for a sample pattern, follow up promptly with a short thank-you letter, the pattern, a good press release (see Chapter 10, "Publicity"), plus your catalog of other products, price list, order form, and phone/fax/email information.

Follow up a week or so after sending the sample, to ask whether the shop has received it. If not and plenty of time has elapsed for it to be delivered, offer to send another one.

If you don't hear back a few weeks after the buyer has confirmed receiving the pattern, follow up by phone to ask how she liked it and if the shop is ready to order.

## Selling to Distributors

Rather than selling one pattern to one customer, or a dozen patterns to one retailer, designers can sell a dozen dozen patterns to one distributor. The distributor then finds twelve shops to buy a dozen patterns each; and each shop, in turn, finds twelve consumers to buy your patterns.

### Distributor Price Formula

Distributors typically pay designers 35% of the suggested retail price for patterns (see page 54).

### Is It Worth the Discount?

An extra 15% discount over wholesale sounds like a lot of money to give up. Why not go after retailers yourself and keep that money?

When I started my business, I went after individual shops. First of all, I had to identify them—find names and addresses, confirm buyers, etc., as described above—which took a lot of time. Then I had to send a letter, promotional materials, and a sample pattern. More time, plus money for postage and the cost of patterns. Then I had to follow up, because only 5% of the shops responded to my letter. Yet more time, plus telephone expense. And when I did get them on the phone, half told me they only buy through distributors because they don't want to keep track of a zillion different vendors; and the other half had lost my packet, could I please send another one? More time, materials, frustration. Then, when those who were interested finally ordered, it was only three-to-six patterns. At $.50 to $1 profit per pattern, that's not much of a wage for all the time and expense I invested. And I still had to invoice them. And then 40 days later, call half to remind them that their payment was overdue. And then call back in another few weeks to ask how sales were going and if they'd like to re-order (shops tend to forget to order from small suppliers).

So, is it worth paying the extra 15% to distributors? My answer is a resounding YES!!

Distributors will save you time, paperwork, and frustration. You'll make more money (net revenue) than you can possibly earn by keeping that 15%.

They'll also pay you within 30 days—pretty much guaranteed. In my experience, distributors are a very low credit risk.

They'll increase your sales volume significantly. They have contacts, a sales force that follows up regularly with retailers, and far more clout in collecting on invoices than a small designer ever will.

And most retailers appreciate consolidating their orders with a few distributors versus keeping track of hundreds of vendors.

Does it sound like I have a strong opinion on this topic?

## Who Are the Distributors?

There are lots of distributors for sewing, quilting, and craft patterns. Check the phone book, the Web, trade magazines, etc.

The best place to find them is at trade shows, such as those listed in Appendix F. Distributors regularly cruise the booths at these venues looking for exciting new products and to talk with designers in person.

Despite the effectiveness of trade shows for meeting distributors, it is possible to get a distributor's attention without going to one.

## The Approach

If you're working by mail and phone, approach a distributor the same way you would a retailer (see page 60). In other words, know the name of the buyer, know what kind of merchandise the company carries, introduce yourself with a letter and sample before phoning, and craft your sales pitch in terms of how your pattern will boost the distributor's business. Appendix G lists some of the major distributors and contact information.

Distributors can be very tough to crack. Most represent lots of products in addition to patterns. They're deluged with requests from designers. They've already got lots of great patterns that are selling quite well, thank you. How to break through?

Sometimes you just plain can't. No matter what you do, they ignore you. Sometimes you can get their attention by sending them a sample. When I was trying to get the buyer at Target to call me back about KinderKakes™, the thing that got her to call immediately was sending a made-up 'Kake, attractively wrapped in a big bakery box, and delivered via personal messenger. Yes, it was expensive. But for an important customer, it was worth it.

Other times you can breach a buyer's defense with creative networking. For instance, if you get calls from retailers to buy your pattern directly because their favorite distributor doesn't carry it, encourage them to ask the distributor to pick it up. If a salesperson gets enough requests from customers for a particular pattern or line, they'll pass a strong message along to their corporate buyer.

Similarly, encourage consumers to ask at their favorite store for your patterns. That's often all it takes for a shop owner to give serious attention to a pattern, and in turn, to ask their distributor for it.

Once you've built up momentum this way, you'll find that the distributors are calling you (yes, it does happen!).

## Exclusivity

The reputable distributors understand that you will try to place your patterns with as many distributors as you can. Retailers often have a strong preference about who they like to buy from. The more distributors that carry your pattern, the more retailers will buy and the more consumers will see your pattern. If a distributor asks for exclusivity, just say no. It's not a reasonable request.

## Following Up

Sometimes when you haven't heard back from a distributor, it's simply because your letter has gotten lost in the pile. Buyers are human, too. So if it's been a few weeks and you haven't heard anything, follow up.

Different people prefer different methods of contact. Some love the phone; others prefer email; still others like faxes. Whatever medium you use for your first follow-up, ask what their preference is for future communications.

Of course, sometimes when you haven't heard back from a distributor, it's because they don't want to deliver bad news.

## Handling Rejection

Inevitably, you'll be rejected by one buyer or another. Be gracious. While rejection is hard on the designer, it is also hard on the buyer. She doesn't like telling you she can't use your patterns, no matter what the reason.

And understand that her reason can be anything from "poor quality" to "great pattern, but I just don't need another of that type right now." If an explanation for the rejection isn't offered, ask (but only if you can handle criticism gracefully). If the buyer liked your pattern but can't use it now, ask if you can resubmit it in six months to a year.

The bottom line is, do your homework and submit the very best product you can to the right distributors, along with a short but compelling argument how they will benefit by carrying your line. If your quality is good and you are professional, don't be afraid to persevere for a response. But gently.

### *Doing Shows*

I've mentioned shows as great venues for selling your patterns to consumers, wholesalers, and distributors. They're pretty big and expensive undertakings, though, so let's talk a bit about how to do them efficiently and effectively. The next five pages include two sidebars with specific advice from trade-show veterans.

### Being There Without Being There

I'll say this first to get it over with: While having your own booth at a big show has huge potential for building your business, you don't have to do them to be successful. Some people (like me) simply don't have the personality for it. You can still have your patterns at shows by getting wholesalers and/or distributors to feature your models and patterns in their booths.

You might also be able to work out a joint promotion with one or more manufacturers. For instance, at the Spring 2000 International Quilt Market, Mountain Mist displayed a dozen of my Humbug Bag™ models in their booth, adorned with tags giving the booth number where the pattern could be purchased. In exchange, I recommended their GOLD-FUSE batting for making the product. (Note that my belief that GOLD-FUSE is an excellent batting came first; then I approached Mountain Mist

about a joint promotion. Don't endorse a product just for the promotional possibilities.)

Enough said about being there on coattails. What about having your own booth?

### Display Models & Samples

If you decide to go for it, display plenty of models in your booth. Have sample patterns available for people to take apart and examine. Design your booth to be attractive and inviting, so it calls out to fast-moving passersby: "Stop here. I've got something you'll like!"

### Offer to Ship Patterns

Bring lots of patterns to sell; but also offer to ship them directly to customers after the show. Many people appreciate not having to carry them home.

### Do a Class or Demo

The difference in show sales with and without a demo and/or class can be quite significant. Whenever possible, teach a class or two to build awareness and promote sales of your products.

### Bring A Smile and Comfy Shoes!

You'll be standing for two, three, or four days straight, meeting hundreds of people. Your goal is to make each of them feel that they're the most interesting and important person in the world to you at that moment… and not to let on that your feet and back are killing you.

Be sincere and helpful to the folks you meet. They'll appreciate it. Make them feel welcome in your booth. Don't badger them to buy something, but be available to answer questions.

And let them talk if they want to. You may be surprised at what you learn!

# Spending Wisely at Shows

*by Ann Anderson, distributor and publisher, QuiltWoman.com*

Quilt Market is the show I know best, but I'll bet what I learned there applies to most large trade and consumer shows.

First of all, shows can be a huge expense in a small designer's budget so it is important to spend your money wisely. Before springing for your own booth, attend the show as a visitor. Even better, volunteer to work in someone else's booth (including set up and tear down) to get the hang of how things work.

## The Booth

When you feel confident you can handle your own booth, then you need to decide how best to spend your money.

- *Booth size and location*

  Not surprisingly, bigger booths cost more money. A full-booth is typically 10"×10"; but you can get halves, doubles, triples, etc., to economize or increase space as needed for exposure and/or budget. Corner- and end-booths are available, usually at a premium.

  Bigger booths give you more wall space. Corners and ends cost more; don't give you as much wall space; but do give you more exposure from different angles.

  Make your decision based on what you are selling and your budget. Personally, I have seen new designers do quite well with just a half-booth, so don't feel that if that's all you can afford it's not worth it.

- *Displaying models*

  Do you want to hang items from the drapes in your booth (versus displaying them on tables, pedestals, floor displays, etc.)? If so, order extra piping around the perimeter of the booth to hang your own drapes. The drapes that are typically provided will not support your models.

  This implies, of course, that if you want to hang models from drapes (i.e., the "walls" of your booth), you'll need to supply your own. Personally, I use a stick-and-mesh system that works well for me. Use whatever works best for you.

  If you prefer to display models on tables, pedestals, etc., bring your own or see if the facility can rent you something suitable. (Editor's note: Check Appendix I for display-stand and rack suppliers.)

- *Carpet, tables, and chairs, oh my!*

  Let's face it; you'll be standing for a long time. Designers who do lots of shows bring their own well-padded carpet. It's as much for comfort as design.

  I use foam-interlocking flooring from Popcorn International (see Appendix I). It's lightweight and inexpensive to ship, and adds immensely to comfort. Typically, you can also rent extra padding for carpet from the show organizers.

  The booth will probably come with one undraped table and two chairs. If you want the table draped, rent one or bring your own. If you bring your own, it must be fire resistant. If you want additional chairs or tables, you need to order them.

  For both carpeting and table drapes, having your own can be a real money-saver if you do more than one show.

- *Lighting*

  This varies from exhibit hall to exhibit hall, so you may want to wait until you see the space for yourself to place your order. If it's a dark booth, you may need to rent lights to spotlight your models.

- *Electricity*
Amazing—but if you need it, it must be ordered at additional cost.

- *Cleaning*
Again, amazing that this is an extra. You can hire to have your booth cleaned each night, or if you have access to a vacuum cleaner, you can do it yourself.

Those are the basics. If you need something else, it's probably available for a price—everything from solid display walls to furniture to plants to podiums and more. Just ask the sponsor.

For most shows, you will need to sign a contract roughly five months before the show opens. You'll be given a set of rules and deadlines, as well as a "decorator package," to arrange for services and rent items for your booth. It's all optional, but chances are you'll need at least a few of them.

## Shipping

Shipping can be as expensive as booth rental. If you can transport all your models and display supplies by car, you will save a bundle. Of course, that's not always possible. When it's not, you will pay for shipping three times:

- First, from your location to the convention center or the convention center warehouse. Ship early enough to use services such as UPS or FedEx Ground instead of paying premiums for faster shipment.

- Second, you will pay "drayage," which is the cost to move your items from the convention center loading dock to your booth. There is generally a fixed rate per

hundred pounds. 101 pounds will cost the same as 199, so pay attention to the weight. It is possible to pay as much in drayage as it cost to ship your items to the center.

Tip: Don't have anyone send an overnight package to you at the show floor; even an envelope will be charged at the 100-pound rate. Most halls are run by union rules, and drayage charges are not negotiable.

- Third, you will pay for shipping back to your home/warehouse. There will likely be a service charge for handling your outgoing shipment from the exhibit hall. You may be required to have an existing account with a major shipper. It is a good idea to set up an account with UPS, FedEx, or another biggie before you go to the show. (Check which carriers pick up from the convention center.)

You can save money by carrying your booth contents from the hall and taking them to an off-site carrier-counter. If you don't have the means (a car and help) or the items are particularly large and/or heavy, just take a deep breath and pay the charges. It's often well worth it after four days of hard work!

## At the Show

At some halls, union rules prohibit the use of wheeled vehicles (e.g., luggage carts) inside the hall, so check the rules before wheeling stuff in. Even if you use a shipper for most of your booth, you still might carry what is reasonable. For example, I like to ship booth decorations and literature, but hand-carry display models.

The exhibit facility will have a vendor-service area staffed with knowledgeable people who can provide you with whatever

*(continued on next page)*

services you need. If you have questions, ask them. If you need something for your booth, request it. I have found that the people working in the service area are generally very helpful.

## Miscellaneous Trade-Show Tips

- Catalogs and brochures are heavy. Bring enough but not too many, to avoid shipping leftovers back home.

  I have found that 500 is a good number, unless your items turn out to be really hot. If you run out, you can take names and mail them later.

- In my opinion, "Sample Spree" is the best "extra" on which to spend your money at International Quilt Market.

- It's worth the expense to have two-part NCR (No Carbon Required) order forms printed. Then you can give one copy to your customer and keep the other. When things get busy in the booth you will find the time savings to be a life-saver. (See page 103 for an example.)

- Bring several clipboards so you and your helpers can follow customers around in the booth, noting patterns and quantities as you go.

- Have a specific place on your order form to note the form of payment (cash, check, credit card, or terms) and whether the items were taken or are to be shipped. Many customers prefer not to carry their purchases, or to take one and have the rest shipped. When you get back home, you don't want to be wondering over every order form what they took and what you need to ship.

- Bring a tool kit. I recommend a hammer, screwdrivers, pliers, stapler, tape (masking, cellophane, and packing), scissors, hook-and-loop tape (e.g., Velcro), safety pins, straight pins, glue stick, marking pens, paper, self-adhesive labels, and any other items specifically needed for assembly of your booth or for hanging/labeling samples. If you're displaying flat fiber-artworks, such as quilts, bring extra hanging sleeves for those that aren't properly outfitted.

- Make your booth inviting. There is an art to creating a wonderful display. Check books on the subject, or better yet go to a show and observe for yourself. What draws you in? What gets your attention?

- When staffing a booth (your own or helping another), be friendly. Don't sit behind a table working on something. Stand up, say "Hi," and try to catch the eye of the customers walking by. Remember you are selling.

  But don't be pushy, either. They're looking for benefits—products that will fill their own needs to make a profit, build customer loyalty, etc. Be sincere in helping them to fill those needs.

- Wear grubby clothes for set up and tear down; it's hard, dirty work.

- And finally, have fun! Get to know your neighbors in the hall; you may find some great new friends.

# Booth In A Bag™

*by Susan Purney-Mark and Daphne Greig,*
*designers, authors, teachers, and Web retailers, Patchworks Studio*

We consider Quilt Market a must for our business. It gets our patterns in front of quilt shops, distributors, and fabric manufacturers from around the world.

But getting booth decorations to Market can be a challenge when travelling by plane and across national borders.

We came up with our Booth In A Bag method originally because we were nervous about the cost of shipping across the Canada-U.S. border. (We've since learned that it's very simple and not expensive.) At our first couple of markets we weren't sure what to expect, so we chose to go with minimal decorations and work upwards from there. We also wanted to be very portable—so that with two suitcases each, we could walk out at the end of Market within 20 minutes of closing.

While most people ship props and decorations commercially, we take everything we need in four suitcases and check them as baggage on our flight.

We select suitcases with specific criteria in mind. Each must have sturdy wheels, semi-hard sides, and can be locked. We check the weight allowance for every airline we will be flying, so as not to incur excess-baggage costs.

## In Our Carry-Ons

We're careful that our carry-on bags are the correct size to fit under the seat or in the overhead bins. We carry on a laptop and one bag (plus purses). Our carry-on bag contains:

- Booth confirmation information and all paperwork concerning our trip

- One wholesale order form—if our suitcases don't arrive on time, we can get these photocopied at our destination. (In fact, we like to do the photocopying at the destination because it saves weight in our suitcases.)

- At least 50 colour catalogs (more if we can fit them), so we'll have something to hand out if our suitcases are delayed

- One copy of each pattern we are showing at Market

- 25–30 credit-card slips

- Purchase-order book

- Business cards

- Customs documentation
  Since we are traveling from Canada to the U.S., we visit the local Customs office before we leave. We show them the quilts we are taking with us and they give us documentation to certify that we are taking our quilts out of the country and will be bringing them back, so there are no problems when we return home.

- Personal medications

- Cameras

- Notepads and pens

- Books or magazines to read

## In Our Checked Luggage

In our (checked) suitcases we pack:

- The quilts we will be showing in the booth. Each one has a label with our name, address, and telephone number.

Each quilt is rolled and wrapped in a sealed plastic bag. We don't want anything getting wet! Be sure to take the

*(continued on next page)*

quilts out of their plastic encasements when you arrive and shake out the wrinkles.

- Café curtain rods to hang our quilts at Market. These collapse and can be placed diagonally in our largest case. We tape them together and put them between two layers of quilts and clothes. S-hooks are available in most conference centres to support the quilts on these rods. (Check beforehand if you need them.)

- Colour catalogs, credit-card slips, and purchase-order books

- Credit-card imprinter, pens, straight- and safety-pins, stapler, scissors, packing tape

- Products for Sample Spree (patterns, pattern samples, bags)

- Small first aid kit (Band-Aids & such)

- Wooden stands for displaying patterns (in our experience, Plexiglass display stands often arrived cracked)

- Artificial greenery for decorating

- Clothing and toiletries (We travel light. A jumper or suit with several tops is our typical choice. *Very* comfortable shoes are a must. We pack toiletries inside zippered bags to avoid damage from spills.)

- Travel iron (most hotels have irons, but this is insurance)

- Pamper-yourself supplies: a bubble bath is great after a day in the booth. Don't underestimate how hard it is to be on your feet, and on your best behavior, for 10 or 12 hours!

In general, we always put the heaviest items at the wheeled end, and spread the weight evenly among our four suitcases.

## General Trade-Show Advice

We use the services of the decorating companies associated with Quilt Market to provide skirted tables and carpet for our booth. We can't imagine trying to take a carpet!

[Ed. note: Many vendors do—or at least they take/ship carpet padding for ergonomic comfort. For instance, Ann Anderson of QuiltWoman.com brings lock-together foam squares, which are easy to pack, ship, and install; see Appendix I.]

- Stay at a hotel on the Market shuttle-bus route so you don't have to worry about transportation.

- If you are working a booth alone, "buddy" with another vendor to accommodate bathroom and food breaks.

- Hire someone to handle cash at Sample Spree so you can chat up the customers; the convention centre can direct you to appropriate staff.

- Always have business cards handy for any moment they're needed.

- Befriend a person who lives in the city you are visiting, if possible. We have a "woman in Houston" who meets us at the airport, helps with booth setup, and makes sure we eat a nice meal at the end of each day.

## Bring a Smile!

Finally, don't forget to bring your *smile* and *enthusiasm* to the trade show. They don't take up any space in your bags—and are invaluable assets in your booth!

# Chapter 9
# Advertising

Advertising is a message that you pay for. Its purpose is to build consumer awareness and establish a distinctive image for your product and/or your company.

Image-building takes time. Typically, results from advertising cannot be measured except over several years. Many people think that advertising will increase short-term sales and thus are disappointed when they don't see a big volume bump the week after their first ad runs. But that's a misconception. Advertising effectiveness can't be measured by short-term sales.

Advertising builds sales over the long term by making people aware that you exist and building their confidence in your products and professionalism. To do its job, advertising needs to be both consistent and sustained: consistent so that the message is easily recognized as "you," and sustained to give it time to work. That could mean a year or two running ads in every issue of several publications before the world acknowledges that you're "real" and can be trusted.

Let's look at the two main categories of print advertising: space and classified. (I will assume that most small publishers aren't in the market for TV or radio ads or billboards. But heck, if they make sense to you, go for it!)

## *Space Advertising*

This is what most people think of when you say "advertising": Paying for space in magazines, newsletters, newspapers, event programs, co-op mailings, Web sites, etc., to print words and graphics whose purpose is to build recognition, image, and awareness of your company and your product(s).

In my opinion, you need to advertise for at least a year in a venue to judge whether it's working, or whether your dollars would better be spent elsewhere.

## Be Consistent

Be consistent in your space ads. Use the same format, typeface, design, and graphic elements in all your ads for the duration of a campaign. (A campaign can be two months, two years, or forever, depending on "reach" and "frequency"—advertising lingo for how many people see your ad and how many times.)

With sufficient exposure, people will come to recognize your company/product without having to read the ad. This is a *huge* achievement, even though it seems counter-productive that they're not reading your ads anymore! When you reach this point, it means people have accepted you as a real business, here to stay. That type of recognition will often be the springboard for a significant growth-spurt in your business, because you've entered the realm of the trustworthy simply by letting them know, month after month, that you exist. (Assuming, of course, that you haven't become recognized for un-trustworthiness. Advertising can't help you with that.)

By being consistent with your advertising, you help customers to know where to look when they want your product. Think about the ads in your favorite magazine. Many of them are from the same company month after month, right? The product may change, but the company identity shines through. If you need something from one of those companies, you know exactly where to go for ordering information.

That's what image advertising is all about. And it usually takes at least several years to reach that place (and several years of wondering whether you're throwing your money away on advertising, I might add). It's hard to keep spending money on advertising when there's no tangible proof that it's working. But such is the nature of image advertising. It's a long-term deal. You have to give it your best shot, and then trust that consistency and exposure will work their magic.

## Identifying Possibilities

It's easy to find places to advertise in print. Just go to the library or magazine rack to see what publications fit your product. Where are products similar to yours advertised? That's often a clue to good possibilities. Ask colleagues what works for them. Ask current advertisers in the magazines you're considering how it "pulled" for them; most will be delighted to share results and recommendations.

Note that there are "trade" and "consumer" publications. Trade pubs address the wholesale/distributor audience; consumer pubs, the mass-market public. These are two very different audiences in terms of the message you need to deliver. A trade account (e.g., a retailer) may be persuaded to buy your pattern with an ad that promises to attract customers to their store and/or sell related products (i.e., the stuff it takes to make your pattern). A consumer may be attracted by a pattern that helps them to use up their fabric stash. Keep your audience's objectives in mind when writing ads (which of course should feature product *benefits*).

## Who's Your Audience

Is your objective to sell direct to consumers? Or are you aiming toward 100% distributor sales? Choose your advertising vehicles based on your target audience.

If your objective is to mass-market patterns, then distributors are your major target customer. That means placing trade-pub ads that highlight how your patterns add excitement and profits to the distributor's business.

If you're aiming for direct-to-consumer sales, then you need to advertise in consumer publications, to tell how your pattern will satisfy their particular wants and needs.

## Deciding Where

Once you've identified the possibilities, ask each publication for advertising information.

Most magazines and newsletters have the names and numbers of their ad representatives listed on the masthead (the column of fine print, usually in the first couple of pages and on the left). When you express interest in advertising with them, they'll mail you a packet that includes a rate card (sizes and costs of ads), a sample magazine, statistics about circulation, the demographics of their audience, etc. Use these numbers to figure out if the cost is reasonable for the number of subscribers, and whether their subscriber demographics overlap your own target-market sufficiently to justify the expense.

Space advertising ranges in cost. Prestigious international consumer publications can cost thousands of dollars for a even a small ad. Multiply that by four, or six, or twelve issues a year, and you're talking serious money, generally out of the league of a beginning pattern publisher. So start small and work your way up to the big leagues.

Don't overlook some of the more specialized publications. Their circulation will be smaller, and since circulation is a big factor in the price of ads, they'll probably be more affordable. If it makes sense for you,

## Why Advertise?

*by Mary-Jo McCarthy, designer and retailer, Southwest Decoratives*

It took me seven years to become an "overnight success." And I attribute much of that success to consistent and sustained advertising.

I believe it's important to include paid, continuous advertising in your budget. If you want consumers to know you exist, you need to tell them—over and over again.

Advertising is like investing in the stock market: While immediate results are often non-existent, it still is the best way to help your business grow over time and to build name recognition in the marketplace.

In my experience: Don't rely solely on distributors and shop owners to promote your pattern line. Despite their best efforts, you'll get very little market exposure.

Advertise! Often!! And advertise in publications that relate to your product, both consumer and trade.

Start small, with black and white ads. Build up the size and add color as your business grows.

For the best return on ad efficiency, sign the longest term contract possible. That way, if you decide to cancel part way through your contract, you'll be charged the difference between the lowest rate and the rate you've backed out on. If you initialy sign the shortest contract with a publication and then decide you want to continue with more issues, you'll pay a much higher overall rate.

Advertise in a publication at least four issues before you decide to cancel due to non-response. Marketing pros know it takes buyers a minimum of four times to see an ad before they recognize and act on it.

Wholesale and distributor buyers are much more apt to try a new pattern company when they see the company's name in print. Running ads in several publications represents your commitment to your business. The fact that you're willing to "spend money to make money" speaks volumes to buyers.

advertise once a year in a show program; these opportunities can be very affordable.

You can reach a national or international audience by advertising in lots of local publications. For instance, most chapters of the American Sewing Guild publish newsletters. You might be able to advertise in all of them—effectively reaching a national audience—for less than the cost of one ad in a big national magazine.

There are a few on-going co-op ad programs. FabShopNet, for instance, will get your letter-size flyer to 2,500 independent quilt shops for a fee ($400 as of this writing) if you supply the flyers (360-892-6500; www.fabshopnet.com). Checker Distributors will deliver your flyer to all their retail customers for free if you supply the flyers (if they carry your patterns, of course).

Consider putting together your own co-op programs. If your pattern requires a particular product, suggest a partnership with the manufacturer to share costs for an ad that features both of your products. (Or even better, convince them that they should feature your product in *their* advertisement.) The same goes for re-sellers of your pattern: Perhaps shops will feature your pattern in their weekly newspaper ad if you offer to share the cost. Or a distributor might share the cost of a trade ad.

## Classified Advertising

Classified ads are the small-print listings that appear (generally) at the end of a magazine. These are far less expensive than space ads; some publications even offer them free to members/subscribers. Opinions vary regarding their effectiveness. Certainly they're less effective than space ads at establishing identity, although consistent use of classifieds could build awareness.

Classifieds are most often used as the "qualifying" step of a two-step ad: The classified offers a free catalog and/or coupon and/or information about a product. The follow-up mailing contains the pitch that closes the sale.

Classifieds are rarely successful at getting consumers to purchase a product directly. There simply isn't room enough to describe product benefits sufficiently to convince them to send money.

## Web Advertising

Don't overlook on-line advertising. (I'm not talking about banner ads, which I don't think are effective.)

Quiltropolis—sponsor of many fiber-arts email lists—offers "daily sponsor ads." In my own experience, these can be very productive for not a lot of money. (As of this writing, they're $5 per ad per list per day; email Beth Ober at betho@quiltropolis.net, or call 301-515-2539, for details.) These types of email lists tend to be highly targeted, even if relatively small in number; so the "conversion rate" (more advertising lingo—the percentage of people who see your ad that actually buy) is often excellent. And satisfied customers on one list will often be great word-of-mouth advertisers for you on others.

# Chapter 10
# Publicity

Publicity includes all the things you can do to get free "advertising." Press releases are a standard publicity vehicle, as are trunk shows, TV appearances, and feature writing. Use your imagination to come up with fun ways to get other people to spend their time and money promoting your business. Publicity is cheap and effective!

## *Press Releases*

Every magazine and newspaper in the country has space they need to fill on a regular basis. You'd better believe they're delighted to get information they can use.

Did you know that much of what you read in publications has been lifted wholesale from press releases written by the designer/manufacturer/distributor/etc.? If your story is worthy of a publication's empty real estate, you'll get free press coverage.

How do you write a press release that gets picked up?

### Target, Target, Target!

To write an effective press release, take off your designer hat and put on a new one: that of a staff writer for the publication you're targeting. Now write!

Avoid the temptation to tell an editor how great your pattern is. Rather, talk about how it solves a problem or fills a need for the publication's subscribers. Mention your pattern as a natural part of that discussion.

To put on the staff-writer hat, you need to know the publication well. That means reading several issues to get a feel for style, the kinds of topics covered, the audience, etc.

Some publications, such as newspapers, are similar enough in audience, style, content, etc., that you can send the same press release to many publications. Others, such as specialty-market magazines, are so specific in their audience and focus that you may need to write one press release for one publication. Yes, it's more work. But it's also more effective. In my experience, it's well worth the extra effort to send strictly targeted press releases.

## Scatter-Gun Serendipity

Writing a press release specifically for a publication is most effective. Still, every once in awhile the "scatter-gun" approach works—i.e., writing a generic press release and sending it to a zillion editors, hoping enough will pick it up to make your effort and expense worthwhile.

A generic release forces the editor to work harder (she has to figure out how it fits into the pub, and then she has to edit it). But if something in your press release piques an editor's interest sufficiently, and she's having a good day, she might just make the effort.

I once scored *really* big this way—to the tune of 60 consumer orders per day for three weeks, with a bell-curve order-profile continuing before and well after the peak (in fact, I still get orders from this "ad" today, six years later). So I'm not about to pooh-pooh the concept. Still, it's neither predictable nor dependable.

Note: If you score with the scatter-gun approach, you reap rich information about your target audience. And often it's stuff you never suspected. For instance, I discovered there was a religion component to my target demographic for KinderKakes™ when I sent press releases to an unknown but promising publication. I would never have thought religion was a factor worth considering in selecting advertising and promotional venues for this pattern; but it was. Be sure to include such intelligence about target audience in your marketing plan. (see Chapter 6, "Will It Sell?")

## Finding Likely Pubs

Chances are you know (and subscribe to) most of the publications in your interest area. Consider sending press releases to other types of publications, too. My favorite resource for discovering unknown possibilities is *Writer's Market*, published annually (see Appendix J). If a description sounds good, then I go to the library to read a few issues and figure out how to approach them.

## Trade & Consumer Press Releases

I write two sets of press releases for every pattern: one set for trade use and the other for consumers. And I often write several press releases per product within each of these categories, each written with a specific publication in mind (remember: target, target, target!).

For instance, for Humbug Bag™ I wrote five trade-oriented press releases, each with a different slant. Their titles/subtitles:

- Humbug Bag™ Is A HOT Seller: Retailer Reports "I Just Can't Keep This Goofy Little Pattern In Stock!"

- Spark Creativity with Low-Risk Projects: Two New Patterns Take the Fear Out of Being Creative

- Humbug Bag™ Pattern Is Exceptional for Teaching Machine Quilting: Help Your Customers Overcome One of Their Top-Three Sewing Fears

- What's In It For Me?: Focus on Benefits, Not Features, to Sell More Sewing Machines

- "Gift Clubs" Build Loyalty and Profits: Give Your Customers a Compelling Reason to Come Back Every Month, and Watch Your Sales Skyrocket!

Each of these was slanted toward a particular publication's audience; each was designed to maximize the odds for getting published by a specific delivery vehicle.

And that's the essence of writing a press release that will get results: Phrase it in terms of the benefit to the customer. (Yup, benefits again!) If the press release is for a trade publication, talk about building store traffic, enhancing customer satisfaction, and increasing sales and profits. If it's for a consumer magazine, talk about easy-to-make, fun, satisfying, improving skills, and/or receiving praise from others (e.g., when giving a hand-crafted gift).

## Content and Format

A press release that I actually wrote and sent is reproduced on the next two pages. (It was printed virtually verbatim by the targeted trade magazine as a full-page "article," complete with color photos. All for free. And readers couldn't tell that it was written by me rather than a magazine staffer.)

There's nothing magic about my format. Feel free to design your own, as long as it includes all the essential elements in the proper order, as described below.

For more on press releases, read the excellent SBA (Small Business Association) article at www.on-linewbc.org/docs/market/mk_release_pr.html

### Introductory Information

Start your press release with three things:

- The phrase "Press Release" or "News Release"
- Contact information, i.e., who to ask if an editor need answers to questions; include phone, fax, mailing, and email alternatives
- The phrase "For Immediate Release" or "For Release On/After (date)" so the editor knows when the information can be published

[Keep in mind that magazines often work on a six-month lead schedule. So if your press release contains information that is time-sensitive, send it six months before you'd like to see it in print.]

### Title (& Subtitle)

Next, a title. I'm a firm believer in using both a title and subtitle for each press release. I figure if one doesn't grab an editor, the other might. I like to use a short title with a longer, more descriptive subtitle. In my experience, editors usually come up with their own titles for articles, so I consider titles and subtitles a way to get the editor's attention rather than something that's likely to appear in print.

It doesn't have to be obvious from your title (or even the introductory copy) that the "article" is going to promote your pattern. In fact, *not* making it obvious often increases the appeal to an editor. A press release should look like it's providing solid information that's of high interest to the publication's audience. Eventually the article gets around to why your pattern is essential to delivering the promise laid out in the title/lead. But you don't have to hammer it home in the first sentence.

### Body Copy

After the title, then the copy. Write it so the most important stuff is at the beginning. If space is limited, editors typically start at the end and lop paragraphs off until the article fits. The exception is the final paragraph, which contains contact and order information; it will generally survive an edit.

Your "lead" (first paragraph) should address the promise of your title/subtitle. If you promised to get them more customers (a typical trade promise), then explain in the first paragraph how you'll do it. If you promised a quick-and-easy gift (a typical consumer promise) explain upfront how your pattern delivers.

Some of the best material for press releases will come from customers. For instance, a reviewer wrote that my Jambalaya™ pattern contained the best instructions for foundation-piecing that she had ever seen. So what do you think my next press release included? Yup!

The best thing about using quotes from customers, reviewers, etc., is that the claim/recommendation/superlative is coming from someone who has no vested interest in the

**Make It Easy** ®
**SEWING & CRAFTS**
2012 Queen Avenue South
Minneapolis, MN 55405-2350

612-377-7560    612-377-7561 (fax)
email (preferred):  nancylynne@aol.com

# NEWS RELEASE

**For Immediate Release**
**Contact:** Nancy Restuccia

# What's In It For Me?

### *Focus on Benefits, Not Features, to Sell More Sewing Machines*

When a prospective customer asks about a sewing machine, do you immediately launch into "the spiel"—in other words, all the things this baby can do? One of the most common pitfalls in selling, no matter what the product, is to talk features rather than benefits.

"Features" are charactertistics of the product, what makes this item different from another. "Benefits" answer the customer's question, "What's in it for me?"

For instance, a feature of your top-of-the-line serger might be the chainstitch; one benefit of that feature—what it means to your customer—is that it can stitch strong straight seams in half the time of a conventional machine. A feature of your best-selling conventional machine might be a special gear mechanism that delivers extra piercing power at slow speed; one benefit is that your customer can sew heavy fabrics such as multiple layers of denim or leather with ease.

It quickly becomes obvious, when you go through the features-benefits exercise, that for a given feature, there can be many benefits. The serger chainstitch feature noted above, for instance, also has the benefit of expanding your customer's decorative-stitching capabilities, among others. Some benefits will matter to a particular customer, others will not. That's where listening and asking probing questions becomes important. What kinds of sewing does this customer like to do? What kinds of fabrics do they typically work with? Have they ever thought it would be nice to be able to         ?… fill in the blank, based on the different benefits you know you can deliver with different machines!

Once you've figured out what benefits a particular customer is most interested in, *show*, don't just tell. Assuming your demo machine is set up and ready to stitch perfectly (and they all are, right?), let the prospect try the technique in order to experience the benefit for themselves. Also important, show samples of finished projects that use the features they're interested in. After all, the customer is buying the ability to make great finished stuff; showing them made-up projects is far more memorable and persuasive than looking through a pile of stitched scraps!

— MORE —

## Back-Door Selling

Don't limit your sales efforts to the person who walks through the door shopping for a machine. There are lots of opportunities to create interest among people who aren't actively looking, yet can easily be persuaded to trade up. Again, demonstrating benefits is the key to turning these types of prospects into buyers.

Perhaps the best way to succeed at such "back-door" selling is through classes and demos. Choose projects that will clearly show the superior benefits that your machines can deliver. This will ensure that your machines shine, leaving all those who aren't using them anxious to try them out.

Two brand-new patterns from Make It Easy Sewing & Crafts® are excellent choices for demonstrating a variety of machine capabilities, leading to back-door sales of machines— not to mention, incremental sales of supplies and notions:

- *Humbug Bag*™ is a whimsical twisted tote that takes its unusual shape from a traditional 19th century English candy. Easy enough for kids to make, and simple enough to complete in a two-hour class. This pattern is great for demonstrating machine quilting (both grid and free-motion), use of the serger for finishing raw edges as well as for decorative stitching (e.g., chainstitch, coverstitch, flatlock), plus a whole range of machine-embellishment techniques from embroidered motifs to appliqué to ribbonwork.

- *Pocket Scribbler*™ is a handy little notekeeper that fits in pocket or purse, briefcase or glove compartment. The cover of the "Book style" version is an exceptional small canvas for demonstrating machine-embellishment techniques using a conventional machine and/or serger, from appliqué to scribble-stitching; also perfect to spotlight an embroidered motif. The "Pad style" version is magnificent made up in leather (real or synthetic)—great for showing off your machine's ability to handle tough fabrics with ease.

*Humbug Bag*™ and *Pocket Scribbler*™ were designed, written, and published by Nancy Restuccia, owner of Make It Easy Sewing & Crafts®. Ms. Restuccia is author of *Quilting by Machine*—a best-selling volume in the Singer Sewing Reference Library—as well as many other popular sewing-and-crafts articles and books, including the "five-star" (Amazon.com) *Hold It! How to Sew Bags, Totes, Duffels, Pouches, & More*. Retailers may order these and other Make It Easy products from their favorite distributor.

### # #

*(August 2000)*

PHOTOS: Digital photo files, ready for print, are available upon request.

product. That makes it a far more persuasive message than if I had said the same thing. It's not advertising hype; it's a "testimonial."

Testimonials often make your press release more appealing to magazine editors. If possible and appropriate, I include at least one quote from an independent party in every one I write. It adds credibility to my promise, and when published, it makes the article look like a staff writer has interviewed several sources for their information.

So save all your customer feedback. You never know when a comment will fit perfectly with the message you want to convey in a press release.

In the last paragraph, list any credentials that support the value of your product (relevant awards, books you've written, etc.). And don't forget to end with ordering information, so folks who have been convinced by the article can purchase easily. Include the postpaid price, Web-site URL, address for mail orders, phone and fax numbers, etc.

### Spacing, Pagination, Etc.

- Double-space your press releases and leave at least one wide side margin, so that an editor can easily edit. It's great if you can fit everything on one page, though I'll admit that I've almost never been able to do that.

- Unless there is a very compelling reason (e.g., free project instructions) don't exceed two pages.

- To indicate that your copy continues on a second page, end the first page with

    —MORE—

  centered at bottom. Start the second page with the page number centered at top, e.g.,

    —2—

- For sending to magazines and newsletters, print on only one side of the page. Include identifying information at the top of the second page, flush right or left.

- Date your press release following the final paragraph (you can also begin a press release with a date), positioned flush right.

- Indicate you're done by typing either

    ###   or   30   or   —END—

  centered below the final paragraph.

## How to Send

Send your press release to the correct editor by name. Getting the person (and the correct spelling) right will enhance your probability of getting published. Call, check their Web site, or look at their masthead to find the right person.

If you can't get a name, add an attention line that will get it to the right person. For instance, if you've written your press release for a particular column within a specific publication, address it "Attn: *Potpourri* Editor."

PRWeb is an on-line service that delivers your press release to lots of recipients for free (www.prweb.com). Personally, I haven't used them because their categories haven't fit my products. But yours might.

## Results

You never know where a press release will lead. I once sent a press release targeted to a particular trade magazine. Sure enough, they published it virtually word-for-word, looking for all the world like an editorial—two pages, full color! A major sewing-machine company's director of education happened to read it and called to ask if they could feature my patterns in classes their educators were putting on around the country at major consumer sewing expos. (I said yes.)

## Extending Their Use

Traditionally, press releases are for sending to the press. (Duh!) I also use them for other things. For instance, I include them in the packets I send to customers who ask for information about a pattern. (Trade releases to wholesale customers; consumer releases to consumers, of course.) For these usages, I typically print on both sides of the page since they're reading, not editing.

## TV Appearances

Every designer wants to know how to get on TV. There are many shows (particularly on cable) devoted to sewing, quilting, and crafts. How do you get to be a guest on, say, The Carol Duvall Show or Simply Quilts (both on the HGTV network, www.hgtv.com)?

Beth Ferrier offers her insights after being on TV twice (see sidebar, next page). Also check out the article "Marketing Via Television" by Karen Combs in the Summer 2001 issue of *The Professional Quilter* (Appendix E).

Keep in mind that many shows are taped live. You don't get a chance to re-do something if you mess up, and you get cut off if you run long. This can be unnerving to some.

## Word of Mouth

This is the ultimate in low-cost and effective publicity. It's simply your customers telling their friends to buy your patterns, how great your service is, how clever your designs are, how fantastic your instructions are, what fun your project is to make, etc.

Word-of-mouth "advertising" costs you nothing, and it's the most persuasive message you could possibly send.

In my experience, the only way to get great word-of-mouth advertising is to produce exceptional-quality products and deliver outstanding customer service. You can't buy it; you have to earn it.

Consumers are typically glad to share their recommendations for great products with friends. Teachers can be excellent advocates for you because they see lots of students and hold a position of authority. Pattern testers will often spread the word for you. Since they have invested their own time in helping you make it a great pattern, they are often very enthusiastic fans, and will recommend it to consumers as well as their local retail shops.

Word-of-mouth advertising is a two-edged sword, though. If your pattern isn't great—if it has mistakes, is incomplete, hard to follow, etc.—you will suffer from negative publicity. People talk, particularly on Internet discussion groups. So build top-quality into your patterns.

## Web Links & Directories

If you have a Web site, links and directory listings are worth pursuing.

### Links

Linking is when another site includes a "hyperlink"—a button, logo, or other icon representing your business—that, when clicked, takes the prospect to your site.

Links are a good thing. Depending on the search engine, lots of links can get you listed higher in the results of a search. Lots of links may also help you get listed with Web directories (such as Yahoo). Some Web sites include a page devoted exclusively to links for just this purpose: to rack up numbers. If you opt for lots of links, be prepared to keep them up-to-date.

Two sites with good and extensive links:

- www.quiltwoman.com/sp_links.cfm
- www.quiltsquiltsquilts.com

Ask permission from a site before linking them from yours. It's not only polite, but increasingly becoming a legal necessity (i.e., if you link to a site that is not flattered by the association, they can sue). Also, be sure to link (jump to the other site), rather than copy (place a duplicate on your own site). Copying someone else's site (or parts of one) is copyright infringement and thus legally actionable.

The most common way to get links is to suggest a reciprocal link, i.e., if they add your link to their site, you'll add theirs to yours.

You can check to see what links exist to your site using a search engine. In AltaVista, for instance, type link:www.yourname.com (substitute your URL for "yourname"). You'll get a list of all the sites that have links to yours. Check on-line for the search protocol for other search engines.

# So You Want to Be in Pictures?

*by Beth Ferrier, designer, author, and teacher, Applewood Farms Publications*

Only the exceptional quilter in this modern age has not seen one of the many televised quilting programs today.

Making a guest appearance on a national television program can introduce you to a wide audience of quilters—many of them your potential customers. As a quilting professional, the exposure can be very valuable. So how do you get yourself in front of the camera?

Let me offer a few suggestions:

• Watch the program on which you'd like to appear. Pay attention to their format. Note the number and length of individual segments. Pay attention to the style of the host and the type of projects they like to feature.

• Send in a proposal that is consistent with the program's format, style, and project preferences. Think of your proposal as a handshake: an introduction to what you do. Keep the topic specific and focused—an outline of what you want to cover.

• Include a resume and samples. Spotlight what makes your technique special. They see lots of "me-too" proposals; let them know why yours will stand out.

• Quilters (and other fiber artists, for that matter) are always looking for the latest innovations in design and techniques. If you've got one, the show's producers want to know that!

• Include copies of your published works, if possible. Although, if you're already a quilting household name, this probably won't be necessary. (Then again, if you are already a quilting household name, you are probably not reading this.)

Urban legend has the appearances can cost you anywhere from $5000 to $10,000. That has not been my experience; I have never paid a fee. I have had to pay for all of my own expenses, though.

## Improving Your Odds

No matter how good you might be at your craft, if the right people have never heard of you they can't know what they are missing. As in any industry, it's not just what you do, it's who you know.

Whenever possible, introduce yourself to the host of the program. While they often don't have final say on who appears, they can influence the pool of choices.

Networking at the large quilting events (e.g., trade shows) is a very good way to make contacts that can lead to a television appearance.

Be persistent. Just because your proposal was rejected this time does not make it valueless. "No" often means "not now" rather than "never."

For me, it was wicked awesome fun to tape the television programs I've been on:

• Kaye Wood's Quilting Friends, PBS, segment 911

• Simply Quilts, HGTV, segment 718

The hosts (Kaye Wood and Alex Anderson) were gracious, generous, and kind. The television crews seemed to be there to make me shine.

My two appearances are a wonderful addition to my resume. And I have truly enjoyed my 15 minutes of fame.

(Note: Most shows list contact information at the end; many have Web sites that tell you how to propose an appearance.)

## Web Rings

Web rings are a variation on links. A Web ring is a group of sites that are linked in a chain, set up and managed by a "ringmaster." Visitors to any site in the chain can travel around the ring in any direction, sequentially or randomly, by clicking on the Web-ring icon (usually at the bottom of the page). Typically, the sites in a ring are related thematically, so visitors to one site can find similar sites without knowing their names.

## Directories

Some sites are exclusively, or contain, directories. If you belong to a trade organization, for instance, be sure to check their Web site for the opportunity to be listed in their directory. Web directories typically don't charge for a listing but they may screen for relevance. A few examples:

- Fab Shop Net (trade organization); www.fabshopnet.com
- QuiltWoman.com (directories, e.g., for designers, teachers, shops); www.quiltwoman.com
- Quilt Index (directory of on-line stores); www.quiltindex.com

Search the Web for many other possibilities in all classes of trade.

## *Writing, Teaching & Lecturing*

Essentially this is publicity piggy-backed on other work—often *paid* work. Writing magazine articles and/or books, speaking to groups, and teaching classes all offer the opportunity to publicize your pattern line.

Your writing/teaching/lecturing topic doesn't have to be about your pattern line. Whatever your subject matter, the venue itself is an opportunity to mention that you have patterns for sale. When writing magazine articles, this often is a short credit (including how to order) at the end. For speaking engagements, it might be that the sponsoring organization offers your patterns for sale in the lobby.

When teaching, it might be selling them after class.

If your primary objective in writing/teaching/lecturing is to sell patterns, be clear before signing a contract that you'll get the credit/plug you require to make it worth your while.

While many writing, teaching, and lecturing opportunities pay something, often it's not much. So if your reason for doing them is to publicize your pattern business, the question to ask yourself is: Is this a great place to advertise my business? Will this raise awareness and help establish image for my business? Will it promote sales of my products?

Personally, if it's the right audience with plenty of prospects and I get to promote my patterns, I'm willing to accept low-pay in exchange for the advertising value.

## *Trunk Shows*

Trunk shows come in two flavors: a personal show-and-tell of your models (e.g., at a consumer show), or sending the models off to be used consecutively by a number of customers (generally retail stores) in whatever manner they deem most appropriate. The latter is the one most designers wonder about.

The reason to do either of them is that models sell patterns. A shop that has models on display might sell three or six dozen patterns; without a model, the same shop might sell half a dozen. Models are a significant sales-booster.

## Timing & Shipping

For trunk shows that travel to individual shops, each shop typically keeps your models for three to six weeks. When the time is up, the shop pays the postage and insurance to send models on to the next shop on the list.

Include a letter/contract with your samples detailing how you want them sent (e.g., Priority Mail, UPS), whether you want the package insured (and if so, for how much), and any special packaging instructions (e.g., enclose samples in a waterproof bag).

## Promotional Requirements

Let's face it. The only reason for a designer to absorb the time, risk, and money to ship models to shops is to sell more patterns. Lots more. So you might want to include some guidelines for retailers as a condition of receiving your trunk show. For instance, you might require that your models be prominently displayed, that your pattern be featured in a class, and/or that shops host some sort of special event around your models/patterns while your samples are on loan to the shop.

## Consigning Patterns

Some designers include consignment patterns with trunk shows. The advantage is that retailers have more patterns in stock than they might be willing to purchase outright. So if demand exceeds expectations, the patterns are on hand and can be sold.

The disadvantage of consigning patterns is that retailers have no real incentive to push consignment inventory through to consumers. Heck, they haven't invested anything; so why should they spend time or money to promote incremental sales?

Still, when samples are on display, you will always sell more patterns than if not. So it's often a good risk to consign patterns with trunk shows.

Personally, I think the best compromise is to require purchase of two or three dozen patterns in order for a shop to get your trunk show, and then to consign an additional two or three dozen patterns.

## Contracts

Trunk shows require a good bit of coordination on the designer's part; but they can also be very worthwhile in boosting sales. A good contract (not necessary to have a lawyer, just need to be clear and complete about your expectations) is a necessity. Also, be clear upfront what the value of your samples is, and thus what you will bill the shop if they damage or lose them. Get signatures!

## Packing Tips

A few suggestions for packing models safely for a road trip:

- Use a sturdy box. Department-store shirt boxes and flimsy cardboard boxes will quickly be destroyed. (My UPS guy told me that the typical package travels through something like 75 miles of conveyor belts and numerous trucks, planes, etc., before reaching its destination. It's a tough couple of days for your precious cargo.)

- Pack your models in a waterproof bag. Rain happens and boxes get left outside. Other boxes can leak and/or people can spill things. Though it's not good to store fiber-based models in plastic long-term, it's cheap insurance for short-term shipping.

- Put something substantial (e.g., a hefty piece of cardboard) on top and on bottom of your models before sealing the box, so there is no danger that the person opening it (with knife or scissors) will slice into whatever's pressed against it, whichever side they open.

- Include a packing list that details contents (checklist-style is helpful). Then everyone knows what you think they've received and what you expect to get back. Any discrepancy between the list and contents can be reconciled immediately, while it's still possible to track down missing models.

- Include your address and the recipient's name and address inside each box (on a card or on the packing list) just in case your outer label gets obliterated.

## *Donation Requests*

Once your business gets known, you'll start getting requests from organizations (such as sewing, craft, and quilting guilds) for donations to be given as door prizes at their major events. It's just like junk mail: The more donations you give, the more requests you get.

To pursue these opportunities without waiting to be asked, just get in touch with the event organizer and volunteer a donation. I guarantee your offer will be accepted!

In exchange for a donation, the sponsoring group generally offers to:

- Print your company and/or pattern name in their event program
- Give you credit when presenting the prize (although anyone who's ever been to these events knows that often the donor is not well-acknowledged when prizes are given)
- Distribute your catalog or flyer to attendees (or set them on a table for people to pick up).

Should you do it?

Personally, if the organization offers to distribute my catalog/flyer to all attendees, I do it. I figure it's a cheap way to get my message to a highly desirable audience. All it costs me is paper and postage, plus the expense of the prize. How many dollars would it take to reach this same audience via traditional advertising?

The prize you donate deserves some consideration. While it's nice to give an actual product (i.e., a pattern), tastes vary. I've personally won two door prizes in my life (a book and some hand-dyed fabric) and neither of them held any appeal for me. How many other people get door prizes that simply don't suit their style or taste? I'd bet a fair number.

I recommend sending a gift certificate for one or more free patterns in response to door-prize requests. (Unless you have only one pattern; in which case, send the pattern.) A gift certificate accomplishes two good things:

- It lets the winner select the item(s) they like, so they're more likely to be pleased and feel goodwill toward your company.
- It forces the recipient to visit your Web site or peruse your catalog, which exposes them to your entire line.

If you adopt this approach put an expiration date on your gift certificates, from three months to one year from date of the award.

## Personal Communications

This is totally free publicity: Include your name and contact information in all communications, such as the signature line of emails (particularly when they're going to targeted e-lists), on letterhead, business cards, flyers, etc.

Absolutely positively include your catalog or flyer with every order you send out! Let customers know the other patterns you have. A current satisfied customer is your most likely future customer. Make it easy for them to place their next order and/or to pass product and ordering information along to a friend. Consider adding a promotional offer (see Chapter 11) in the envelope, too, to give customers an incentive to order again right away.

You might also consider publishing an email newsletter. A regular newsletter reminds prospects that you exist and that they like your products. It also gives you a qualified database of prospects to email new-product announcements to.

If you decide to do this, include folks who've purchased your patterns as well as ones who ask to be put on your mailing list. Don't make it just an advertisement for your products, however. Give them substantive information and/or some giggles. Ami Simms' monthly newsletter is a good example of this advertising tool. Last I checked, she had almost 10,000 people signed up to get her newsletter. (To check it out, go to www.groups.yahoo.com; from there, choose "Hobbies & Crafts," then choose "Crafts," then "Quilting," then "Ami Simms Newsletter.")

## Trade Shows

Trade shows are primarily a venue for selling your patterns. But they also can be a publicity vehicle. You can network and get your name and products in front of lots of people at trade shows. They're also good places for picking up related gigs (e.g., writing and teaching). And for meeting fabric and notions manufacturers to work out joint promotions. And for gathering market research on trends and the competition. "Why I Love Quilt Market," by Beth Ferrier (next page), describes some of the many benefits of doing trade shows.

# Why I Love Quilt Market

*by Beth Ferrier, designer, author, and teacher,
Applewood Farm Publications*

Sure, I'd prefer to have distributors sell my patterns. It takes about the same amount of time to ship off 100 patterns as one. You do the math. Even if I'm getting a smaller cut of the pie, it's a much bigger pie.

Even so, I firmly believe in hosting my own booth at International Quilt Market. If all you ever want to be is a pattern designer, then having distributors carry your patterns is just fine. Yours will be one of hundreds that shop owners can flip through in the distributors' booths, along with all the other distractions of the market.

People learn about my patterns in my booth. Sometimes they buy from me, some times they buy from one of my distributors. But they buy. And they do that because they saw my quilts hung out in all their glory. They learned specific information about each pattern. They get to open the pattern and see all the diagrams. They learned about the great support that I give with teaching guides, supply lists, and clip art.

And if you have other aspirations beyond just writing patterns, listen to this: The distributors come to your booth. You don't have to go, hat in hand, looking for the buyer. They come to you.

And so do the fabric companies. I can't tell you how many yards of fabric will be showing up at my door in the next month. And I get to have it before even the shop owners get to see it. So I will be having two different fabric companies cross-promoting my patterns in spring and fall next year.

And so do the program chairs for guilds. I have three new teaching/lecturing engagements in the works. That will more than cover the cost of Market.

And so do the magazine editors. They are always looking for designs, especially from people with some reputation in the market. It is a great way to gain exposure for your work.

And so do the catalog buyers. And they are the real backbone of my business. They generate a lot of my income.

The networking alone is worth the cost. I have been amazed at what I can learn by "allowing" someone to just rattle on. Yikes!  I've met some pretty powerful people.

If you want to be "real" in this market, get yourself a trade-show booth!

## Chapter 11

# Promotion

Promotions encourage a sale *now*. Promotions provide an incentive for increasing short-term volume—for getting prospects to say, "Yes, I'll take one today."

Promotions typically offer a deal with a deadline (date or quantity) as an incentive for quick action. Some examples:

- Discounts, e.g., 10% off any order placed this week
- Get one free, e.g., buy three patterns and get a fourth free during May
- Package deals, e.g., Show special: buy the entire collection for $50 and save $15
- Premiums, e.g., buy three patterns and get this (handy notion) free, while supplies last
- Sampling, e.g., try it, you'll like it; and no obligation if you don't (offer expires 1/1/03)
- Frequent-buyer programs, e.g., after buying 12 patterns (over time), get a 13th for free

Promotional offers fall into three categories: trial, increased-purchase, and continuity.

*Trial promotions* aim to get new customers to try your product. Free samples are the most powerful tool for gaining trial, *if* your product is good enough to convince consumers to come back for more. Demonstrations and in-store models are also excellent trial-builders.

*Increased-purchase promotions* provide an incentive for customers to buy more than they had intended. Get-one-free and package-deal promotions are good examples. A consumer may have intended to buy only one pattern, but your deal to "buy the entire collection and save $10" is too good to pass up, and they end up with eight patterns.

*Continuity promotions* aim to ensure repeat business and build a purchase habit. Frequent-buyer programs are a good example: giving customers an incentive to continue purchasing from you. Premiums can build continuity, too. For instance: Collect one item of a set with each monthly purchase. To get the entire set, the consumer must purchase a product every month.

Use your imagination to come up with unique and compelling promotions that will help you achieve your business objectives best.

There are state and interstate commerce laws regarding promotions. If you offer a promotional price to one customer, you must offer the same advantage to all other customers in that class of trade. For instance, you can't give Checker Distributors a better price than you give United Notions. But you can give all distributors a better price than wholesalers or consumers; they are different classes of trade.

Some considerations for specific tactics:

## Discounts

Discount offers can range from a specific dollar savings ("Save $10 when you purchase the entire line") to a percentage off ("20% off") to throwing in something for nothing ("Free shipping with any purchase"). Discounts reduce the total the customer pays.

Discounts can be used to increase the number of items purchased ("10% off purchases over $20"); or to encourage trial ("50% off"); or to build continuity ("An additional 2% off each month when you order every month for a year").

Since it's cheaper to ship more patterns than less (less labor and shipping) it makes

economic sense to offer volume discounts. If a consumer orders three patterns versus one, or a distributor orders eight dozen versus five, a promotional discount can easily pay for itself.

## Free Samples

A free sample is the ultimate in trial promotions. What could be more compelling to get non-customers to try your product than to simply give it to them?

But sampling is expensive. And it only works if your product is good—sufficiently better than competitive offerings that trying yours will convince a prospect to buy. If you have a me-too product, forget sampling.

It may make sense for you to offer free samples to some classes of trade but not others. For instance, I think the volume potential of a distributor always justifies the expense of giving them one or more free patterns. For wholesale accounts (e.g., retail shops), I'd gamble that the risk/expense of sending a free pattern will be worthwhile. I'd also give a free pattern to any teacher who is sincerely interested in trying it. But for direct-to-consumer sales, sampling is a more questionable strategy for getting new customers.

## Freebies on Web Sites

A low-cost vehicle for delivering free samples is as downloadable files on a Web site. A warning though: Don't give away the store! Give just enough to demonstrate the quality of your work. If you give too much for free, consumers will balk when you ask them to pay.

Several designers I know have offered mystery quilts, given out in monthly installments on their Web site. Each installment was free for the month it was introduced. After that, if a customer wanted it, they had to pay for it. Once the whole quilt had been published in this manner the entire pattern was available for purchase. All of this was clearly spelled out on the site. And in theory it's a great strategy for building traffic and establishing a monthly site-visit habit. In theory.

What actually happened is that consumers who missed an installment (or two or ten) got upset! They didn't want to pay for something that they could have gotten for free (even if it was their fault they failed to take advantage of it). So they demanded the entire pattern, even years later. Outrageous as the situation is, it's no-win for the designer. If she says no, the consumer thinks she's being unfair; if she sends patterns for free, she'll soon be out of business.

Another designer offered projects free on her Web site while preparing her line of for-sale patterns. The theory was to build awareness and traffic to the site early, so that when she introduced the pattern line there'd already be a bunch of folks who liked her work and visited her site regularly. Again, good in theory but not so good in actuality. Consumers were insulted at suddenly being asked to pay for what they had been getting for free.

Another danger in offering freebies is that many folks think that if it's free, they can take it and do whatever they want with it. So they copy it for friends, put it on their own Web site, use it as a class handout, etc. Obviously, this is not okay. So include a clear copyright explanation on everything you offer free. I use the following; feel free to adapt it for your use.

> A note about copyright: Copyright is a hot topic these days among small publishers like me. I believe that most copyright violations occur with generous intent but lack of understanding. Please repay my kindness in offering the "free stuff" on this site with the kindness of respecting the following guidelines: I invite you to print out the information on these Web pages for your personal use. Feel free to refer your friends to my site so they can print out their own copies. But please do not reproduce and distribute your copies without my permission—that is a violation of my copyright. If you want to copy and distribute my work to other people (including class handouts and reprinting in other publications), email me at nancylynne@aol.com and explain your situation.

Bottom line: Think carefully about freebies. Personally, I think having one free project to demonstrate the quality of your instructions is sufficient. Beyond that, the only two types of freebies I would offer are:

- Tips and techniques that can be used in conjunction with your patterns (or not)
- Galleries showing your pattern projects made up in other colors, sizes, etc.

## Contests, Sweepstakes & Lotteries

In a contest, winners are chosen based on skill. They may be charged an entry fee, or required to use your pattern. In a sweepstakes, winners are selected by random drawing; no entry fee is required. Lotteries are like sweepstakes except they require a fee to enter.

If you're thinking about any of these, understand that there are strict legal requirements that vary by state. If you sell patterns to customers outside your state, that's interstate commerce and makes you subject to federal laws governing contests, sweepstakes, and lotteries. Check with a good lawyer before fielding any of these.

## Joint Promotions

This is exactly what it sounds like: a promotion that includes two or more partners.

For instance, a manufacturer might be willing to include a coupon for your patterns inside their package; that adds value to their product and gives consumers an incentive to buy yours. Perhaps, together, you could offer a rebate when a consumer purchases both of your products and sends in the UPCs.

You might be able to talk retailers into giving their customers a discount when they purchase your product plus one or more others. They'll likely more-than make up the discount in increased sales volume. Suggest that they merchandise the two, three, or four products together in an end-cap or check-out display—hog heaven in promotional terms!

Joint promotions offer lots of creative possibilities. Personally I think they're very exciting, and underutilized in the fiber-arts industries. What might you put together with another manufacturer that would help both of you increase sales?

## Shop Models

Models sell patterns! One retailer says, "If the designer loans us samples, we'll order lots of patterns—usually at least 36 because we will kit a good sample immediately."

Consider making multiple models and offering them for sale to shops. This works best for quick-and-easy projects that can be reasonably priced, of course. A shop owner is not going to pay more for a model than the amount they'll profit from pattern sales.

## "Sample Spree"

One of the best venues for selling shop models is the "Sample Spree" sponsored by International Quilt Market. Sample Spree takes place the night before Market opens.

The samples you sell can be shop models—i.e., made-up items, such as dolls or quilts—or they can be sample patterns. As a rule, customers (shops) are far more interested in buying shop models than sample patterns.

If you sell at Sample Spree, include a flyer or catalog of all your products with your booth number prominently featured. Often buyers spend the evening before Market opens planning their strategy for the next several days. If the catalog you give them at Sample Spree piques their interest, they may just add your booth to their "must see" list. (And of course, one way to convince them to visit your booth is with a promotional offer, e.g., a free pattern, a free luggage tag, a discount, etc.)

## Identifying Opportunities

### Brainstorm From Industry Publications

In my experience, one of the best ways to come up with ideas for sales promotions is to read magazines—trade and consumer, in the proportion that matches your business objective—with an eye to finding new customers.

In a recent issue of the excellent trade publication *Sewing Professional/Round Bobbin* for instance (see Appendix E), there was an article written by a high-school sewing teacher. That made me think, "Hmmmm, how could I promote sales of my quick-and-easy patterns to sewing teachers at high schools across the country? Note to self: Talk with several local home-ec teachers to find out how they get patterns for class, what publications they read, and whether they might be interested in using my patterns to teach kids to sew."

Another gotta-have trade magazine, CNA (Appendix E), recently featured a freelance teacher. That prompted me to think, "Hmmm, freelance teachers often use patterns as the basis for a class. Their students are required to buy the pattern. So what do freelance teachers need most? Help getting teaching gigs at shops? Help finding students? Help with class materials, such as handouts, advertising art and copy, tips on step-by-step timing and/or techniques? Note to self: Talk to some teachers and find out what they need most, and figure out if I can give it to them as an incentive to use my patterns for their classes."

Continually brainstorm in this manner (with yourself or others) about markets that can multiply your sale efforts.

### Cultivate Current Customers

Finally, it's worth stating the obvious: Your best future customer is your current satisfied customer. ("Satisfied" is the operative word in that statement.)

When you introduce a new pattern, let your past customers know. Assuming they like your other work they'll buy in far larger proportions, at far less expense, than folks who aren't familiar with your product. Send a postcard or email telling them the benefits of your newest pattern. (Note: Be sure to offer past customers the option of *not* receiving such notices; some folks do not welcome them.)

# Chapter 12
# Tracking & Analysis

Okay, you've done all this up-front strategic stuff to get your business off to a great start: identifying your target audience, marketing your product in terms of customer benefits, figuring out how to reach them efficiently, etc.

So, were you correct in your original assumptions? Is your marketing plan working?

These are questions you have to ask yourself continuously. And you have to adjust your assumptions as necessary to deploy resources most cost-effectively.

## *Tracking*

Tracking means tagging, or coding, each promotional effort so you know what finally convinced each customer to order. Understand that any given purchase may be the result of the cumulative impact of many marketing elements (e.g., an image ad, a word-of-mouth recommendation, and an attractive discount at the local store). Even so, it's helpful to keep track of what actually closed each sale. That informations helps you to figure out where to concentrate future resources for the best return.

An easy way to tag your ads and/or promotions is to add a "Dept. T9"-type designation after your street address. The post office will ignore it; but when you see this code in the address on the envelope, you know that this customer was responding, for instance, to the ad you placed in the September issue of *Threads* magazine.

Code the order forms you distribute, too (e.g., if you send a batch to a guild show). For instance, ASG-Mil-01 could indicate this was one of the flyers you sent to the American Sewing Guild/Milwaukee chapter's annual show in 2001. That enables you to tally orders from particular venues at the end of the year and see whether it's worth your time and money to send them again.

## Analysis

Tracking is useful only if you use the information you gather to make strategic decisions.

Look for patterns (similarities, that is; not sewing patterns). Are a large proportion of orders coming from a particular demographic group? If so, use this information to refine your target market.

For instance, if you get an overwhelming response to an ad in the *AARP Journal* but a mediocre response to the exact same ad in *Parents* magazine, chances are your target audience is older and without small children at home. Use that information to search for other places those same types of folks "hang out" (in magazines, physically, on the Web, etc.).

Include information from your customer database in your analyses, too. (You do keep a database, right? See page 97 for more details.) For instance, if you're getting a disproportionate number of order from one region or country or state, ask yourself, "Why?"

Norwegian designer/publisher Barbara Skjønberg (www.quilt-design.no/index2.htm), for instance, discovered that shops in Minnesota were buying her patterns in significantly larger numbers than most other U.S. states. Why?

The most logical answer is that Minnesota has a large and active Scandinavian community. So what other locations have similar communities? She should go there, too! If her patterns sell as well in those other locations, she can feel confident that she has figured out a key demographic to her own audience appeal. If they don't sell, she needs to go back and come up with an alternate hypothesis, i.e., figure out what other factors might be responsible for disproportionately high sales in a particular location—and then take advantage of that intelligence.

Continually adjust your target-audience demographic and benefits-message based on the results of your promotions and advertising efforts. Effective marketing is a simple matter of zeroing-in on who your customers are and what they want. Of course that's often a moving target; which is what makes the process so much fun!

# Section III:

# Business & Legal Issues

# Chapter 13
# Setting Up Your Business

## *When to Start*

A common question new designers ask is, "Should I start with one pattern or wait until I have a 'line'?"

Certainly it's easier to get picked up by a distributor if you have several patterns rather than one. It's more likely to be profitable faster, too. That's basic economics: Customers can buy more if you've got a larger selection. A multi-pattern line also provides more opportunities for follow-up sales. For instance, when someone buys one pattern, you can send a catalog and/or promotional offer with it that encourages them to buy others.

Even so, there are some good reasons to start selling with your first pattern

- It gives you an idea of what's involved in self-publishing and marketing patterns. If you like it, proceed full-steam ahead; if not, you can bow out fairly gracefully.

- It helps you to establish a loyal following. Folks who buy and love your first pattern will buy your second in very large numbers, even if it's awhile coming.

- It starts building brand-recognition and awareness-of/ traffic-to your Web site, both of which are essential to continued sales.

That said, I personally started with one pattern seven years ago. I did it after my "real" job. And I wouldn't do it differently if I had it to do over again. The customer testimonials alone were worth their weight in gold when going after retail shops and distributors later (see "Press Releases" in Chapter 10). But I didn't even consider going after distributors until I had built up a line of four patterns that had a solid sales record.

## Laying the Foundation

No doubt you've heard of vision and mission statements, business plans, and company-identity programs. But chances are you've never done them. Let me assure you they're not as scary as they sound. And they *are* important to your success and your sanity. They provide guidance when you get bogged down in the details of running your business and can't see the forest for the trees.

### Vision & Mission Statements

These are short statements that characterize your business. When working on new patterns, written vision and mission statements will stand you in good stead. It's all-too-easy to get wrapped up and carried away by a fun idea that doesn't reinforce your business purpose. Vision and mission statements help you to stay on track and build a cohesive image for your business. A cohesive image, in turn, will help you to build brand-recognition among customers, so they'll know what a pattern from XYZ Company will deliver.

### *Vision*

Your vision is what you want to be or become, i.e., the dream. Often, it begins with the words, "To be the best (whatever)…" My vision for Make It Easy Sewing & Crafts® was:

To be *the* place sew-ers, quilters, and crafters look first for gifts to make.

This vision statement was based on market research. I read magazine and email lists, I talked to teachers and consumers and shop-

owners. From that research, I concluded that people who enjoy making things are often hungry for new hand-crafted-gift ideas. That seemed to be a real consumer need—and importantly for me, one that seemed adequately large to build a profitable business around it.

### *Mission*

Your mission statement tells why you exist; in other words, your purpose for being. Like your vision, it should be an enduring statement rather than something that changes every year. The mission enlarges on your vision, providing more specific direction for your company. The mission of Make It Easy Sewing & Crafts® was:

To help beginning- to intermediate-level home sew-ers, quilters, and crafters to enjoy sewing more and to improve their skills and confidence by providing complete, accurate, and easy-to-follow instructions for creating fun and distinctive "I made it myself" gifts for all occasions.

Whenever I got intrigued by a project suited to those with expert skills, this mission statement helped me see that it wasn't appropriate for my brand. (Might be great for a magazine article, though; see Appendix A.)

### Business Plan

A business plan describes how you will realize your vision and mission.

It's helpful to write both a long-term and an annual business plan. The long-term plan (often five or ten years) helps keep you focused on where you want to go. The annual plan helps you focus on specific goals to accomplish each year, and the things you must do to achieve those annual goals (including a timetable).

For instance, one of your long-term goals might be "to earn $36,000 per year profit from selling patterns by 2005." To get there, annual goals for this year might include "to introduce two new patterns" and "to get signed by one major distributor." Strategies and tactics for the year might include getting instructions written by a certain date, scheduling photography, lining up testers, reserving a booth at a show, etc.

Long-term goals help you recognize when to make changes and what those changes should be. It might be to hire employees, or to sell out to a larger firm. Knowing where you're going long-term helps you to chart the appropriate short-term course.

There are many good general reference books on writing a business plan. If you need help, check a business bookstore or library. Your state Small Business Assistance office may offer pamphlets, books, and/or consulting help. There may also be organizations in your area that offer help in writing a business plan, such as SCORE and Small Business Development Centers (often affiliated with colleges). Or you might find course at community colleges that address your needs.

## Company Identity

Your "company identity" is how the public perceives your business. You create an identity in many ways, including your name, your logo, your reputation, and your image.

### Business Name

The easiest business name is your own, e.g., Jane Doe Designs. This approach works best if your name is well known, so potential customers know what a product associated with Jane Doe will be about.

You can also adopt a name that simply describes your products, for instance, Folk Art Dolls or Advanced Appliqué Designs. The obvious advantage of these is that potential customers understand immediately what kind of products you offer.

Personally, I like names that describe the promise of your products. To come up with such a name, go back to your vision and mission statements. Analyze what your promise is: What need are you filling?

When I named my pattern business, I figured that my most compelling strength (and point-of-difference versus the competition) was my ability to write accurate, easy-to-follow instructions. So I named my publishing company Make It Easy Sewing & Crafts®.

Years ago, I named my corporate-writing business Words That Work! because I figured that effective communication was the promise that would attract the most corporate customers. Remember, Fresh Step isn't selling cat litter; it promises a fresh-smelling litter box.

Another approach to naming your business is to come up with something evocative, as described in Chapter 3, "Pattern Name" (beginning on page 30). Please refer to that section for things to consider when choosing a name, and how to find out if a name is already taken. See Chapter 15 for trademark information.

### Logo

A logo can be as straightforward as your company name done up in a fancy typeface or it can include graphic elements, stylized type, etc. Whatever, your logo should convey the feel of your business. If your patterns are contemporary, your logo should look clean; if your patterns are country, your logo design should convey a down-home feel.

Avoid typefaces that are hard to read, as well as designs that are difficult to decipher. It's just too much work for the consumer. Make your logo easily recognizable.

When designing a logo, consider all the different places it will be used: business cards, letterheads, Web site, pattern covers, press releases, invoices, advertisements, etc. Be sure it can work well in all these spaces.

Consider, too, how your logo works in both black-and-white and color, how it photocopies, and how it reads both large and small. Aim for a design that reproduces clearly and crisply in all these permutations.

If you're not an artist, consider using click-art as part of your logo. Traditionally, clip-art (which was physically cut and pasted into layouts) was sold royalty-free; in other words, by purchasing the book, you bought full rights to use the images however you wanted. Click-art (the digital version of clip-art) is generally sold the same way: Purchase gives you the right to use any of the images however you want, including as part of a product offered for sale. But check the rules when you purchase a particular package to be sure of the rights you're buying. This includes click-art offered on-line. Just because it's on the Web doesn't mean you can just take it.

### Reputation

Your reputation is your most important business asset. Period. Never compromise it.

Many things factor into reputation. Some of the most important are:

- The quality of your products.

  Consumers, retailers, and distributors tend to be wary of patterns from independent designers—often for good reason. Many self-published patterns are incomplete, inaccurate, and/or incomprehensible. Establish a reputation for excellent-quality patterns and you will earn a loyal following among both wholesale and retail customers. They'll be waiting for your next pattern, money in hand. And that kind of following is what will enable you to grow exponentially. Always remember, it costs many times more to find a new customer than to sell your current offering to an existing one.

- Your dependability in filling orders.

  This is especially important in dealing with distributors and shops. Fill and ship orders within 48 hours of receipt to establish a reputation for dependability.

- Great customer service.

  Customer service is one of the few things that distinguishes companies these days. How many of your suppliers (from cable-TV installers to Internet-service providers to car mechanics) make you feel like you're imposing when you need something? A reputation for exceptional customer service will set your company apart from the crowd.

  Answer inquiries in a prompt and friendly manner, add the occasional personal comment with an order, be generous when you goof by sending a free pattern, etc. You'll reap tremendous goodwill by doing so, which will translate to word-of-mouth referrals that build your reputations and your business. If you treat your customers like pests, they'll squash your reputation like a bug.

- Honesty and integrity.

  Do the right thing. 'Nuf said?

### Image

Everything you do, everything you send, everything you say contributes to your image. Image is the overall impression your business conveys to consumers. It might be cutting-edge design, it might be folksy chatter, it might be great instruction. Whatever image you decide to cultivate, your name, your logo, your pattern designs, etc., should reinforce it.

As for vision and mission, it's helpful to write down what kind of image you're after, so when you're designing new patterns, coming up with new names, etc., you don't unintentionally veer from your goal.

## Registration

Register your name and/or license your business as required by your state and municipality. Check with your Secretary of State and/or small-business-registration office for the particulars. Often it's neither a difficult nor a costly process. Some municipalities don't require registration for home-based businesses. Others have zoning laws that may limit the type of business you can conduct from your home.

Note that registering your business name with your municipality is an entirely different thing from registering a trademark. See Chapter 15 for details about trademarks.

## Taxes

Yes, you need to pay them, both the income and the sales variety.

### Income Tax

There are three basic ways to structure your business: you can be self-employed (a sole proprietor); you can have a partnership; or you can incorporate. The type you select for your business will dictate how to file your income taxes. Check with your lawyer and/or accountant to see what will work best for your unique circumstances.

Personally, I'm a keep-it-simple kind of person, so sole-proprietorship was my choice. Paperwork is less and easier than with other types. I file a Schedule C with my personal tax return each year, and that's it.

## Sales Tax

If your state has a sales tax, you'll need to register with those folks, too, for two reasons: to pay and to not pay sales tax.

"To pay" pertains to passing along the sales taxes you collect from customers to the state. Basically, you are required to collect tax on in-state retail sales, and then at the end of the month (or year, depending on volume) to send that money to the state. You'll need a sales-tax I.D. number for those transmittals.

When you sell to wholesalers or distributors (who will re-sell your products), they don't need to pay sales tax, as long as you keep a "Resale Exemption Certificate" on file for the customer. When the product is sold at retail, that customer pays the sales tax.

"To not pay" pertains to purchasing supplies that become part of the product you then sell to customers. Printing is such a cost; your computer is not. To purchase supplies without paying sales tax, you need to give the vendor a "Resale Exemption Certificate" or tax-I.D. number.

(Note that the above details apply in Minnesota. Check with your own state's sales-tax office. They'll be delighted to send you lots of information and forms.)

## *Administrative Systems*

You want to spend more time designing than doing office chores, right? That means automating and integrating as much of your record-keeping, invoicing, data analysis, and other administrative systems as possible. The goal is to enter data once, and have it flow automatically to all the places it's needed. For instance, when you enter an order, you want that information to generate a packing list, a mailing label, an invoice, and a bookkeeping entry.

You won't need much firepower at first; but as your business grows, having integrated administrative systems will keep you sane and smart. So even though it might seem like overkill, the time to establish good integrated systems is early in the life of your business— long before you desperately need them. That's when you have time to think about what you really need, and time to learn to use them.

It's helpful to consult a tax advisor/ accountant to help set up your systems, but you can also do it yourself using off-the-shelf software (Intuit's QuickBooks and QuickBooks Pro are highly regarded by those who work on PCs; unfortunately their Mac version is not well recommended).

## Customer Database & Analysis

Every business will have different requirements for their administrative systems. Nevertheless, every designer needs to keep track of who their customers are; where they're located; how to get in touch with them (mail, phone, email); how much, when, and what products they buy; and how they heard about you.

Analyze this data at least every six months. Use it to figure out how to build your business. Does it give you a clue what markets are most productive? which of your advertising/publicity/promotional strategies are working? what types of products have the broadest appeal?

Some things to look at:

- What percentage of business comes from each class of trade (i.e., retail, wholesale, distributors)?

- What percentage of direct-to-consumer sales are by credit card versus check or money order? Are these percentages trending up or down over time?

- Do orders come disproportionately from a specific region/state/city? Are foreign orders a big factor in your business? If so, is there a particular country/city/region they seem to appeal to most? Why? Can you find other similar markets?

- What percentage do each of your titles contribute to total sales? Is it significantly different when you look at sales by units versus dollars?

- How do sales by title stack up by wholesale customer? Do certain customers account for a large proportion of sales of a particular title? If so, why? Can you find more customers like them to sell that pattern?

- Check out sales by month, by pattern. Is there a seasonality component to your business? For instance, do your sales increase just before the holidays? Do different patterns sell well at different times of year?

- For ads, publicity, and promotions, what draws the highest response rates? Is there a publication or audience that your pattern seems particularly to appeal to. How can you reach more of those kinds of people?

- Is there a particular place that gets mentioned again and again by customers when you ask how they found out about you? (You do ask on your order form how they heard about you, right?) If so, consider advertising or promoting there, if possible.

This is not an exhaustive list. Be creative in analyzing your customer database to figure out who other likely prospects are, how to reach them, what services might increase sales, etc.

## Back Up Your Files

Do it! Don't procrastinate!! It's very inexpensive insurance.

Keep a Zip disk close-at-hand. Every time you update your customer database, copy the new file to your back-up disk. Once you have a CD-full or annually, whichever comes first, burn a CD back-up. CD is a more reliable long-term back-up than a Zip.

Keep back-up copies of your patterns in the same manner: short-term revisions on a Zip, and final files on a CD. Archive the graphics and font files in addition to your page-layouts. When you need to reprint, everything you need is in one place (see Chapter 4, "What Your Commercial Printer Needs").

I keep my back-up disks and CDs in a fireproof safe. An off-site depository is even better. Don't store them next to your computer; that defeats their purpose in the case of a physical disaster (e.g., a fire).

## Credit Cards

You'll sell significantly more, with less credit risk, if you accept credit cards. I fought this one for a long time, claiming I wasn't big enough, didn't need it, etc. Then when I finally succumbed and added credit-card capability to my Web site, retail orders jumped 300% within a month. (Oh, yes, crow tastes great.)

The good news for a beginning designer is that you don't have to have your own "merchant account" to accept credit cards. You can use a credit-card (CC) service for orders placed from your Web site.

### Credit-Card Services

The way these services work is:

- Your customer buys your patterns from someone (a company) that has a legitimate merchant account

- The owner of that merchant account then buys the same patterns from you, and asks you to send them directly to the consumer (this is called drop-shipping, a common practice)

- The merchant-account owner pays you for the patterns they bought, keeping a percentage for their role as broker in the transaction

There are drawbacks to using a service. Legally, only the merchant-account owner is authorized to accept credit-card orders. Thus, you cannot take a CC order over the phone, or at a consumer or trade show. Still, if you're just getting your feet wet, it's a good place to start.

CCNow (www.ccnow.com) is one such service. They charge 9% of the total billed cost (including postage). While this sounds high, remember that these are retail-price sales, so you have a lot more wiggle-room than for wholesale or distributor sales. Another service is Net+Catalog (www.netpluscatalog.com).

### Merchant Accounts

If you want to be able to take credit-card orders by mail or phone, or if you do shows, you'll need a merchant account. As a rule-of-thumb, if you're doing more than $400/month in credit-card orders, it's probably economical to get a merchant account.

Costs and equipment vary depending on your needs. Typically you will pay for the equipment/software, plus a monthly fee, plus a percentage of each transaction (often around 2%). Many designers are happy with their merchant accounts purchased through Costco. Bank Card USA in California also comes highly recommended (www.bankcardusa.com; 800-589-8200). Check also The Fabric Shop Network Retailers Association (www.fabshopnet.com; 360-892-6500).

## Business Bank Account

Many designers like to have a separate bank account for their business. It simplifies accounting and looks more professional. And it may be a bank requirement.

I've managed three sole-proprietorships over the past 20 years and have never had a bank deny my deposits because checks were made out to my business rather than to me personally. (I endorse them first with "Nancy Restuccia, owner," followed by whatever phrase the purchaser happened to put on the check—which can be anything from a company name to the headline of an ad!) However, other folks have been required by their banks to maintain a business account in order to deposit checks made out to a business name. So play this one by ear.

If your bank is as open-minded as mine, understand that it is not necessary from either a legal or IRS perspective to maintain a separate business checking account *if* you are a sole proprietor. For the IRS, you simply need to prove that something was a business expense (i.e., keep receipts and justification); it doesn't matter what "pot" you took the money out of to pay the bill. Paying for something using a business-account check doesn't necessarily make it a business expense.

## Where to Turn for Help

As you build your business, you will undoubtedly have questions that aren't answered in these pages. Rest assured, there are places to turn for help and support.

## Email Lists

One of the most wonderful email lists for pattern publishers (and publishers-to-be) is:

- QuiltDesigners. While the focus is quilt patterns, the information is applicable to most any type of pattern. Join from www. groups.yahoo.com (choose "Hobbies & Crafts," then "Crafts," then "Quilting" to get to the list info). Sue Wilkins in Canada (www.quiltseeds.com) is the list "mom"; she and Patti Anderson in the United States (www.patchpieces.com), Barbara Skjønberg in Norway (www.quilt-design.com), and Beth Maddocks in Switzerland (www.piecebynumber.com) brainstormed the idea for this list several years ago to encourage networking, information-sharing, and support for fellow designers/self-publishers. I'm a long-time member and cheerleader. Reading the archives is like taking a course in pattern self-publishing.

There are many e-lists that are not specific to pattern publishing, but offer a broader perspective on your customers and your industry. You can often pick up valuable information to improve your products and services from these lists. Among them:

- **QuiltBiz**: Sign up at http://planetpatchwork.com/quiltbiz.htm
- **SewBiz**: From www.quiltropolis.com, go to "Mail Lists," then choose "Business" and then "SewBiz"
- **A Craft Biz Connection**: Sign up at www.craftassoc.com
- **Friends of Cloth Dolls**: Sign up at www.thedollnet.com

## Industry Associations

Most industries have trade associations that promote their members' commercial interests and provide research and advice that helps them to improve profitablity. The fiber-arts industry is no exception.

Appendix E lists a number of trade organizations. You may find one even more specific to your interest with a Web search.

## Classes and Conferences

Industry associations often hold annual meetings at which they might offer classes on topics of interest to pattern publishers. So, too, trade shows. Check their Web sites for clues about what's coming.

There are many conferences, too, sponsored by for-profit as well as not-for-profit groups. Some are pricey, others are inexpensive or free.

For instance, Dan Poynter (author of the book *The Self-Publishing Manual*) offers free seminars to promote sales of his book (check www.parapublishing.com for details).

The Quilt Professionals Network—a "guild" of professionals from all aspects of the quilting world—sponsors two annual meetings that offer a variety of workshops (see Appendix E for contact information).

QuiltWoman.com threatens to sponsor an annual conference specifically for pattern self-publishers (check the Web site for updates: www.quiltwoman.com).

There are many more opportunities to take classes and attend conferences. Don't limit yourself to a particular industry when searching for possibilities. For instance, your local Small Business Administration office may have just the class you need.

# Chapter 14

# Filling Orders

To get your patterns to customers, you need to have the appropriate shipping supplies on hand; pack them properly; choose the right delivery service; know how much to collect for postage and handling on pre-paid orders; and understand terms and collections.

## Confirming Wholesale (WS) Orders

When you get an order from a wholesaler or distributor, confirm it by phone, fax, or email upon receipt. Let your customers know that it is your policy to confirm orders upon receipt, so if they do not receive a confirmation they know you have not received their order and they should re-send it.

In your confirmation message, include a thank-you, and let them know when you will be shipping their patterns (within 24–48 hours, right?) and by what method (UPS, post office, FedEx, etc.). If it's a huge order and you don't have enough assembled patterns on hand, it's generally permissible to ship a partial order immediately with the remainder to follow within a few days. If you need to do this, you should pay the excess shipping charges.

When selling patterns at trade shows, the easiest way to confirm orders is to use an NCR (No Carbon Required) form and give the customer the copy. Most printers can print these for you. Read more about them on the Web at:

www.goprinting.com/Pages/aboutforms.html

A sample form is reproduced on the page at right. Even though they're relatively expensive per-form (in the 20–25¢ neighborhood for small quantities), your out-of-pocket expense isn't big (e.g., $58 for 250 forms). They're well worth it in convenience and time-savings.

## Schedule Changes

When you will be out of town, give customers plenty of notice so they can order before you leave—particularly for wholesale and distributor customers. Give them at least a week's notice so they can check their inventories and order if necessary. If you will be out of town for an extended period of time (more than a week), make alternate arrangements to keep your business running in your absence.

## Basic Supplies

Most of what you need is obvious: boxes, envelopes, address labels, tape, stamps, etc. If your volume becomes significant, you might want to get a postage meter; but that's advanced pattern fulfillment. This is the 101 course.

You can purchase most of these supplies at your favorite discount or office-supply store. If you're purchasing larger volumes, you might be able to buy wholesale. (You have a resale exemption number, right?) You can also buy mail-order (see Appendix I for several suggestions). Check prices and quality at several places; they can vary widely.

For envelopes, labels, and forms that require a return address, you might also check with a commercial printer. If you order these along with letterhead, invoices, and business cards, you may get a good price on the lot.

## Envelopes

Most consumer mail-orders can be filled in 6½"×9½" envelopes. If your patterns are particularly thick, you may also need to stock 7½"×10½" envelopes to accommodate multi-pattern orders. (Assuming your patterns are packed the standard 6"×9" zip-lock bags.)

If you ship using U.S. Postal Service Priority Mail, you can get envelopes for free (9½"×12½" cardboard). Currently (2001) the U.S.P.S. offers two different envelopes/rates; be sure to use the right one:

- Up to one pound, ships for $3.50
- "Flat rate" ships for $3.95 regardless of weight (as much as you can cram in)

You can order these envelopes to be delivered to your doorstep by calling the USPS supply center toll-free at 800-527-1950. They have a Web site from which you can order (www.usps.com), but I don't recommend it. Go there to determine item numbers and quantities; but place your order by phone. Every time I've ordered via their Web site, I've gotten at least duplicate orders, and frequently three to four times as many things as I've ordered. Although it doesn't cost me anything to get extras, it's a waste of materials, energy, and storage space.

## Boxes & Padding Materials

For wholesale/distributor/catalog customers, you'll need shipping boxes and presentable packing materials. If you're shipping via U.S. Postal Service Priority Mail, you can get free boxes in a number of sizes (see above for Web site). FedEx overnight also offers free boxes, too, although you won't typically need to ship using overnight service.

If you're shipping via another carrier, check your Yellow Pages for a box wholesaler or order by mail from one of the suppliers in Appendix I. (Typically less than half the price of buying the same boxes from pack-and-post type places.) Even though new boxes cost a good 50¢ apiece or more, it's part of projecting a professional image. Don't be penny-wise but pound-foolish.

Four standard-size boxes accommodated my needs for storing and shipping patterns:

**Wholesale Order Form**
***QuiltWoman.com***
26540 Canada Way
Carmel, CA 93923
Toll Free 877-454-7967  FAX 831-624-7132
ann@quiltwoman.com  www.quiltwoman.com

Shop Name _____

Contact _____ Title _____

Address _____ Telephone _____ Fax _____

City_____ State _____ ZIP_____

e-mail_____ Web Address _____ Country_____

Resale Number _____

| Marketing Code | Description | Quantity | Unit Price | Extended Price | Quantity Taken |
|---|---|---|---|---|---|
| | | | $ | $ | |
| | | | $ | $ | |
| | | | $ | $ | |
| | | | $ | $ | |
| | | | $ | $ | |
| | | | $ | $ | |
| | | | $ | $ | |
| | | | $ | $ | |
| | | | $ | $ | |
| | | | $ | $ | |
| | Actual shipping cost will be added FREE shipping for orders of $150 or more | Total without shipping | $ | | |

**Payment Method***
Cash ☐
Credit Card ☐
Check ☐
Terms - Net 30 ☐
*International orders by credit card only

Special Instructions:

Order Taken By_____

Credit Card Type:  VISA  MC  AMEX    Number_____ Exp. Date _____

Billing Address _____ City _____ ZIP_____
(If different from above)

Signature_____ Date_____

QuiltWoman.com Wholesale order form Rev. 1 10/1/99

*Sample two-part NCR (No Carbon Required) form for trade shows*

- 10″×6″×4″ to ship two to five dozen patterns, depending on thickness
- 10″×6″×6″ for eight to twelve dozen
- 10″×10″×6″ for twelve to twenty dozen
- 18″×10″×6″ for storage and for orders of 25 to 35 dozen

Use presentable packing materials: newspaper (age it for two weeks or more so the ink doesn't transfer), bubble wrap, blank newsprint, etc. Don't pad your boxes with odds and ends salvaged from other boxes. (That's just tacky. Save it for mailing stuff to your mom or grandkids.) If you use Styrofoam "peanuts" do your customers a favor by sealing them in bags rather than sprinkling them over the static-prone plastic-bagged patterns.

## Packing Tape

Paper or plastic, it's your choice. Whichever you use, be sure that your package is securely sealed—no loose edges to catch on conveyor belts, no partially-stuck tape to come loose in transit, etc.

## Mailing Labels

You can purchase blank labels on 8½″×11″ sheets at an office-supply store; simply run them through your printer with a logo and return address. Or have them printed by a commercial printer (with your letterhead, business cards, etc.). Or use 8½″×11″ self-adhesive sheets (a bit less expensive than label stock) and get them printed and cut at your favorite photocopy/quick-print place.

## Stamps & A Postage Scale

A small postage scale will make filling orders much easier. They're available in office-supply stores. Get one that weighs at least up to one pound, preferably two. Then you can weigh packages and apply the correct postage yourself. Packages that weigh less than one pound may simply be dropped in a mailbox (as of 9/1/01), saving you a trip to the P.O. on days when all your orders are lightweight.

Keep a variety of stamps on hand in the denominations you most often use. For me that was one-, two-, three-, and four-ounces, plus Priority one-pound and Priority Flat Rate. Stay current on rates for the weights you ship most frequently. You can get a rate brochure free from the post office or on their Web site (www.usps.com).

## Catalog/Brochure/Flyer

You're sending the pattern(s) anyway; so get your catalog/brochure/promotional flyer into the customer's hands for free. With every order you fill, include information that tells them what other patterns you have and that makes it easy for them to order again.

## Shipping Forms

Keep a supply of shipping forms on hand for all of the carriers you use. Fill them out before you leave the office to make your trip to the carrier counter a quick one.

Also keep a supply of international-customs labels (from the P.O.; they're mint-green at left, white at right). Fill them out before you get to the P.O. to make your visit as short as possible. If you typically insure packages, keep those forms on-hand, too.

## Return-Address Stamp

A self-inking return-address stamp often comes in handy.

## *Packing Pointers*

### Storing

When you're assembling patterns, group them into dozens for storage. Most wholesale customers order by the dozen or half-dozen. Counting them out as you assemble them, and then again when packing orders, gives you a double-check on the number of patterns you're sending.

Be accurate in your counts. It tells your customers that you're careful and professional, and will help you build a trusting relationship that will stand you in good stead when you introduce a new pattern or need a business reference. Everyone makes a mistake now and then; but make them as few and far between as possible.

I like 18″×10″×6″ cardboard boxes for storing assembled patterns. They're big enough to hold a decent supply, but not so big and heavy that I can't lift them off a high shelf. You may have something else that works. Fine.

Whatever you put them in, I advise storing assembled patterns standing on their side edge with the zip-locks facing alternately right and left for every group of twelve. Then it's easy to see at a glance how many dozens you have on hand.

## Shipping

When I ship patterns to customers, I pack them with each dozen facing opposite directions so they can easily count the quantity.

Pack patterns snugly. Stuff filler into all empty spaces so patterns don't shift in transit. If your patterns arrive damaged, it is your responsibility to replace them. Don't risk incurring that cost; pack well the first time.

Include a packing list that enumerates the contents of your package and the customer's P.O.#. A packing list facilitates routing and accounting when the box gets to its destination. The customer will check contents against the packing list upon receipt. If there's a discrepancy, they'll notify you immediately.

Packing lists may be included either (1) inside your box or (2) in a plastic envelope affixed to the outside of the box (see Appendix I for suppliers).

Do not include an invoice with your patterns; send it separately. Sometimes boxes don't get opened right away (a good reason to put your packing list on the outside of the box).

Also, it doesn't hurt to put a piece of sturdy cardboard under and over your patterns. That way—whether your package is opened from the top or bottom—your patterns are protected from case-cutter damage.

## Shipping Pointers

Ship the cheapest way that ensures your package will arrive on time and in good shape. Your customers are paying for shipping and will know if they're being overcharged.

## Compare Prices & Services

All the major shippers have Web-site calculators that will give you a good idea of the cost to ship a package. Calculate the estimated cost for each of the carriers, then choose the most cost-effective service. The Web calculators for the big three carriers are at:

- United States Postal Service, www.usps.com; choose "calculate postage" from the menu
- Federal Express, www.fedex.com; choose "rates" from the menu
- UPS, www.ups.com; choose "rates" from the menu

Note that UPS and Federal Express provide $100 insurance at no charge; the U.S. post office charges for insurance from the first dollar. UPS and FedEx also track your packages for free. If these services are important to you and your customer, be sure to add these "extras" to your postal-rate calculation so you're comparing apples to apples.

Costs for UPS and FedEx depend both on weight/dimensions as well as destination; for the post office, distance doesn't affect cost.

Shippers also have different levels of service, ranging from next-day delivery to a week or more. Know what level of service your customer needs, so you don't charge them for services they don't need.

## Rules of Thumb

With experience, you won't need to use these calculators; you will develop a feel for which service is the right one to use. My own rules of thumb:

- For lightweight orders within the U.S., use the post office. (See "International Orders," next page, for packages sent across a border.)

First Class is less expensive and generally as fast as Priority service for packages 13 ounces or less. Over 13 ounces is automatically Priority mail—so go with the Flat Rate Priority envelope if it fits.

- For small wholesale orders (a dozen or two patterns), it's generally quicker and cheaper to use the post office than UPS or FedEx Ground. Consider a Flat-Rate Priority Mail envelope if it's big enough to hold the order.

- For medium-size orders (three to six dozen patterns), use the Web calculators to compare rates. If it's a toss-up, choose either UPS or FedEx Ground for their automatic insurance and tracking.

- For larger orders (packages over six pounds), use UPS or FedEx Ground. UPS generally gives a better rate than the post office, and the relatively new FedEx Ground service is even less expensive than UPS.

## International Orders

Should you accept them? Absolutely! It's easy to ship anywhere in the world right from your local post office.

Collecting payment for international orders is easy, too. Most convenient is by credit card, but you can also receive foreign payments via money order. Simply specify that payment should be in U.S. funds. (There may be small bank fees on both ends for money orders.)

### Fees

Depending on the country, your customer may have to pay excise tax, sales tax, value-added tax, and/or customs duties to receive your package. It doesn't hurt to remind foreign customers that they are responsible for taxes and fees imposed at their border.

There are no extra fees or licenses required to send your patterns out of the U.S.

### How to Send

The most economical carrier for foreign orders is usually the U.S. Postal Service. They offer Global Priority envelopes for free, which accommodate most consumer orders. Rates vary by destination but are quite reasonable ($10 or less to most countries). Check the USPS Web site or your local office for current prices (www.usps.com).

For small orders to Canada and Mexico, International Airmail is a viable and less expensive option than Global Priority.

Other shipping options (UPS, FedEx, and DHL) are generally more costly than postal mail, and often add a hefty brokerage fee to get the package across the border. So the $25 worth of patterns you send to Canada via UPS could end up costing your customer $40 to receive. Check with your customer before using any of these services, to be sure they are willing to pay these additional fees.

## Customs Forms

The U.S. post office requires that you fill out the green and white Customs-declaration form (CN-22). Specify the package contents and value, and the name and address of sender and recipient. Use the description "printed instructional material" and check the "merchandise" box when sending patterns.

Other carriers have their own customs forms, often more extensive.

## Figuring Postage & Handling

Wholesale and distributor customers generally reimburse your actual shipping costs. So that's a no-brainer. But with consumer mail-orders, shipping needs to be pre-paid. That means you have to tell them how much to include before you know what they're ordering.

Many retailers use a sliding scale—e.g., $2 for one pattern, $3 for two, $4 for three or more—to accommodate different-sized orders equitably. Other retailers prefer a flat rate for the sake of simplicity—e.g., $4.75 shipping on all orders. And still others build the cost into the pattern price, and offer "free" shipping. Choose the system that works best for you.

# International Commerce? Yes!

*by Susan Purney-Mark and Daphne Greig,*
*designers, authors, teachers, and Web retailers, Patchworks Studio*

The world is shrinking rapidly. One need only to look at the changes in the European Union and the increasing importance of NAFTA (North American Free Trade Agreement) to see that the world is moving toward eliminating international tariffs and trade barriers.

Our company—Patchworks Studio, established in 1996—is both a quilt-pattern publisher and a Web-based storefront for patterns, fabric, quilt software, and other quilt-related products. As the foremost Canadian quilting site on the Web, we have been selling our products both retail and wholesale to customers around the world for a number of years. We have learned a great deal in the process, and are delighted to share some of the highlights of our experience with you.

We have tried almost every available cross-border shipping method including courier (UPS, FedEx, and others), regular mail, bus, and upon occasion even personal delivery! Our experience has been almost entirely positive. We have never lost a shipment; we have learned from our mistakes; and we are constantly reevaluating and updating our methods. Our current guidelines for cross-border shipping from Canada include:

- We ship Canada Post (regular mail) about 90% of the time. Developing a positive relationship with our local post office has made a huge impact. Our friendly local postmistress is very good about extending us credit, as our fees often run into the hundreds of dollars per month. She volunteers information about the best rates, whether we should add insurance, what expected shipping times are, and lots of other goodies. We have considered a postage meter for the business, but believe we are better served supporting another local small business that looks after our interests so well.

- We rarely insure our parcels except on very high-value shipments or when requested by our customers. We have *never* lost a package! We always ship via airmail, even within Canada. Our postmistress explained that the shorter the time the package is in transit, the less likely it will go missing. Makes sense to us.

- Shipping by courier (UPS, FedEx, etc.). Investigate thoroughly before choosing this method. Couriers offer advantages over regular post, such as Internet tracking, pick-up and delivery at my front door, and monthly billing. However these perks come at a price: higher rates and brokerage charges. When shops outside of Canada ask for courier shipping we explain that they would incur brokerage fees even if the items are NAFTA exempt (patterns and software fall into this category).

For our distributors that want shipping by courier we generally bill shipping, taxes, and brokerage fees separately once we have received the courier invoice.

We do maintain a UPS account. It's very easy to obtain, and especially useful for shipping our booth to trade shows.

Bottom line advice: Take the time to investigate thoroughly your shipping options. Personally, we spent time on a variety of Web sites—UPS, FedEx, United States Postal Service, and Canada Post—and requested rates for an imaginary identical parcel. The difference in costs were significant! You need to balance the money-time-security equation for each shipment and customer.

*(continued on next page)*

*(continued from previous page)*

When shipping internationally, you are required to state the contents and value of the parcel. The Customs Service—or the courier company on behalf of the Customs Service in the recipients' country—determines whether duty and taxes will be applied. In Canada, we pay the Goods and Services tax, a Customs duty, and a service charge (currently $5.00) for any parcel that comes from another country. Those fees can really add up! This can be a significant cost for the consumer as well as your business customers. (Note: If the parcel is a gift from Auntie Jane, then it is treated differently by Customs.)

## Shipping Models to Foreign Publishers

Shipping patterns is one thing. But shipping our precious original quilts is quite another!

We have had to ship these unique and valuable items internationally, and it requires an entirely different set of criteria than shipping easily-replaceable patterns.

Sending models by courier, and insuring them at an appropriate value, translates to staggering brokerage fees. So we send our models through the mail, with piles of insurance on them!

Of course, proper Customs documentation is required. For us, that included forms to indicate that the quilts were leaving Canada to be photographed at our U.S. book-publisher's location, and would subsequently be returned to us in Canada. While the paperwork was considerable, following the proper steps resulted in the actual back-and-forth shipping being relatively easy. We notified our publisher when the quilts were being shipped, they called us upon receipt and we repeated the process upon their return. This method also applies when shipping quilts across the border for quilt shows.

We follow the methods recommended by the couriers and postal services, we fill out the appropriate forms, we pay the required fees… and as a result, we have met with reliable service and satisfied customers. What more can our business expect?

I recommend going with the simplest system you are comfortable with and that covers your costs. If you plan to ship all orders using the U.S. Post Office's "Flat Rate Priority" envelope, then you need to charge everyone at least $3.95 to cover your out-of-pocket expense.

Consider value when deciding on postage and handling fees. If you are thinking of mailing everything Flat Rate Priority, ask yourself if customers will consider it a good value. While it's easier for you, if your pattern costs only $7, your customers may have a hard time justifying $4 for postage.

A sliding-scale system has the advantage of fairness: Customers pay only for the postage required for their order. The disadvantage is complexity; too many levels and it gets confusing.

If you use a sliding scale (and I always did), my advice is to keep it to as few steps as possible. I used two: $10 or less, and over $10 (for U.S. orders). Some customers will pay a bit too much postage and others not enough; but it averages out over the long run.

"Handling" can be added to the price of postage, to cover time spent packing, trips to the post office, etc. But don't get excessive with handling, or it'll look like a revenue stream.

Note that in some states, shipping and handling charges are taxable items. If yours is one, you need to set up your accounting/billing system to include sales tax.

## *Terms*

"Terms" are when and how you expect to get paid. Be consistent! Offer identical terms to all customers within a given class of trade. This is not only a legal requirement, but it reinforces your professional reputation.

## Retail Terms

For direct-to-consumer sales, it's customary to be paid first, then ship the pattern(s). Pricing is at suggested retail price (SRP), except for special promotions.

Some designers wait for a check to clear before shipping merchandise. I believe it's better to ship the pattern within 24 hours of receiving the order, and to take your chances on a bounced check. In my seven years selling patterns, I had less than ten bad checks. People who sew and craft and quilt tend to be honest, salt-of-the-earth types; they're 99.8% trustworthy. I believe there's far more to be gained by extending your trust and demonstrating exceptional customer service than you risk by assuming a check will be good.

## Wholesale Terms

If yours is a sales-tax state, be sure to get the customer's resale-exemption number/certificate before selling patterns at wholesale prices, to protect yourself from having to pay their tax if they don't.

It is customary to specify a minimum quantity for wholesale orders. That's because your discounted price is based on the assumption of saving time, materials, and postage by shipping in bulk. WS minimums for patterns are typically three, six, or a dozen. The minimum can apply to each title, or you can allow "mixed titles"—that is, any combination of patterns that adds up to your minimum.

The advantage of low minimums and allowing mixed titles is that shops are more likely to take a chance on one or three than a dozen. The disadvantage, of course, is that it takes more time and expense for you to fill small and mixed orders.

It is customary to extend "net 30" terms to wholesalers in good standing. That means that full payment is due within 30 days from the date of the invoice. (This is a good reason to get your invoices out on a timely basis.) Some manufacturers offer a discount if an invoice is paid in less than 10 days. Generally this is 2%, and appears on the invoice as "2% 10/Net 30." To my knowledge, this is not a common practice with small-press patterns.

For a first-time customers, check credit references before extending "terms," i.e., the privilege of paying 30 days from receipt of patterns. For questionable-credit customers, get a credit card number before filling the order.

Be sure to specify who pays shipping for wholesale orders. It is common for the customer to pay, particularly on small orders; but some retailers expect free shipping. Be clear upfront to avoid misunderstanding.

## Collecting On Late Payments

Late- and non-payment is a tricky, but unfortunately common, issue for independent publishers—particularly with retail accounts. (Distributors, on the other hand, tend to pay on time). If you are late in receiving a payment, send a tactful first-reminder to the shop, assuming that maybe they've legitimately misplaced your invoice, such as:

Dear Mary,

Could you do me a favor? In checking my records, I see that we have one open invoice for you. It is number 1245, dated 1/13/01 for $89.20. A copy is enclosed for your convenience.

Would you check your records and let me know if you have paid the invoice? If not, would you mail us a check right away. I apologize in advance if this is an error in my bookkeeping.

Hope all is well.

Sincerely,

If that doesn't work, send a second, more demanding letter. If that gets no response, call. Speak to the owner or manager. And if that doesn't get you a payment, consider either taking them to small-claims court or turning over the account to a collection agency (although often that isn't cost-effective).

## Distributor Terms

Distributors buy in much larger volume than wholesalers, so minimums are generally higher; 24, 36, and 48 are common numbers. As for wholesale sales, the minimum can apply to each of your patterns, or you can allow "mixed titles." Personally, I think it's wise to allow mixed titles at these quantities.

Payment terms are the same as for wholesalers: "net 30" for accounts in good standing. Most distributors will send credit references with their introductory materials. Do check; but in my experience, almost all distributors are a good credit risk for small publishers.

Again, be sure that you're clear about who pays shipping. Most distributors are willing to pay shipping, but many have their own systems and rules for doing so. For instance, one of my customers reimburses whatever UPS "should" pay (their judgment), regardless of how I ship or what UPS actually charged me. Another sends me pre-paid shipping labels for their carrier of choice. And yet another adjusts the distributor price to include the equivalent of shipping.

## Consignment

A word about consignment sales; that is, giving a supply of patterns to a wholesaler or distributor, and getting paid for them only if and when they sell.

*Consignment sales to distributors.* A number of distributors work this way. I have never felt "used" by these customers. I have always been paid on time, and patterns and dollars are well accounted for. They don't tie up any more of my inventory than is reasonable. Selling on consignment is simply the way they work and if I want to work with them, that's what I have to do. I have sold thousands of patterns on consignment through distributors. In my book, they're A-ok, and I wouldn't hesitate to work with them on this basis.

*Consignment sales to retailers.* Working with retailers on a consignment basis is a whole 'nuther ball of wax. I don't do it, except under two conditions: I know and trust them, and it's for a big consumer show.

Since there are lots of my target audience at consumer shows, I want my patterns to be there. It's difficult to predict how many will sell, so I'm happy to give a retailer I trust (to take care of my stuff, to merchandise it well, and to pay me promptly) as many patterns as they will take. (Note that if you do this, be sure to provide models to display in their booth. Models sell patterns! You could even offer help setting up, if you'll be at the show; chances are you'll get nice visibility in the booth that way.)

I don't recommend consigning patterns to wholesalers (retailers, teachers, etc.) under any other circumstances. There's simply no percentage in it for the designer. If a shop owner has a pattern on consignment, there's no incentive for them to push it. If it sells, fine; but if not, they aren't out anything. On the other hand, if they've made an investment in inventory, they have a compelling reason to merchandise and promote my pattern.

Also with consignment, there's no urgency about paying the bill (heck, who's to say they sold any? or when?), or to keep the patterns in good shape if they're eventually returned. The upside potential is so marginal on consignment sales, I say, "Don't go there."

## Credit Cards

As mentioned in Chapter 13, you will sell significantly more with less risk and better cash-flow if you accept credit cards. Credit cards also reduce your paperwork and administrative costs. There are fees; but if you're aiming at a mass-market business, they are quickly recovered with savings in other areas.

# Chapter 15
# ©, ™, and Licenses

Let me make this crystal clear: I am not a lawyer. Please do not take anything I say here as legal advice. I absolutely do not offer it as such.

The information in this chapter is based on personal conversations with several lawyers and also on extensive reading. To my best knowledge it is accurate. But I cannot guarantee it. So use this information as a guideline only. Consult a lawyer for specific legal advice.

See the resources listed at the end of this chapter for some great places to learn more about copyright and trademark issues.

## *Copyright*

Copyright is, quite literally, the legal right to copy and distribute original material. The minute you commit your original, copyrightable work to "tangible form" it is copyrighted—whether or not you register it with the U.S. copyright office, and even if you don't have the © symbol on it. (You should do both; but even if you don't, you still own the copyright.)

For works created after January 1, 1978, a copyright lasts for the lifetime of the owner plus 70 years.

## What Is Copyrightable?

The "tangible expression" of "original works of authorship" may be copyrighted. Concepts, procedures, ideas, principles, etc., may not be copyrighted (they might qualify for a patent, however).

For instance, the words and illustrations in Nanette Holmberg's Faux Chenille books are copyrighted. No one else can use the specific contents of her books (e.g., for class handouts, on their Web site) without her permission. But the ages-old idea of stacking multiple layers of fabric, channel-stitching on the bias, and cutting between stitching lines (i.e., making slash fabric, which she calls Faux Chenille) is not within her copyright. Anyone can use that technique in their own original work.

"Useful" objects cannot be copyrighted. Bags and articles of clothing are considered useful and thus are not copyrightable (although design elements, embellishments to the fabric, etc., might be). The concept of "vest" or "tote bag" doesn't belong to anyone; but an original design/piecing instructions/embellishment on either one might be copyrightable.

Finally, public domain property cannot be copyrighted. For instance, if you design a quilt pattern that uses a decades-old block such as Log Cabin, you can copyright the specific interpretation of that block as used in your quilt (colors, arrangement, scale, etc.). But that doesn't give you a copyright for the Log Cabin block concept itself.

## Public Domain

Once a copyright expires, the work becomes part of the public domain—available for use by anyone. Anything published before 1923 is already in the public domain. For later works, check whether the copyright is in force or has expired before using it.

## Five Rights

U.S. copyright law specifies five exclusive rights. If you want to get into the particulars, please refer to the resources at the end of this chapter. In my experience, the essence of these five rights as they pertain to pattern designers is:

- Only the designer has the right to copy and distribute (for free or for a fee) your pattern
- Only the designer has the right to make "derivative copies" of your pattern, i.e., to create something new, but that is clearly based on the original work (for instance, to publish a tip or technique lifted from the pattern as a freebie on your Web site)

There's an old-wive's tale that frequently makes the rounds: If you change a design by 10% then you may claim it as your own. (In other permutations, it's 20%, or two things, or six things, etc.) All not true. The "derivative copies" provision clearly gives the copyright owner—and only the copyright owner—the right to make new work based on old. If it's obvious to a casual observer that one work is based on another, it's a derivative copy.

Note that your legal right to copy and distribute has nothing to do with whether you sell your work or offer it for free. Many people think that if something is offered for free, they can do whatever they want with it. Again, not true. Copyright is strictly concerned with copying and distributing; whether money changes hands is irrelevant to the legal issue.

## Registering Your Copyright

In my opinion, do it! Legally you own a copyright even if you don't register it. But it's inexpensive insurance to do so.

If you choose to register, do it within three months of publication of your pattern. If you don't, you may not be considered to have had the copyright from your publication date. (There is a "group copyright" form which may be applicable if you are publishing several patterns at the same time.)

Registration costs $30 (as of 9/1/01), and gives you two important protections:

- The right to go to court to prevent others from stealing your work
- The right to defend against allegations that you stole someone else's work

The downside to both of these is: Going to court is expensive. Copyright complaints are typically civil suits (rather than criminal), so each party has to pay their own way no matter what the outcome. Which is why some designers elect not to register and simply hope for the best. It's a personal decision.

There are many variations of the copyright application form. The one I use for sewing, quilting, and crafts patterns is Form VA, which the Copyright Office describes as "for published and unpublished works of the visual arts (pictorial, graphic, and sculptural works, including architectural works)." Other options are listed on the U.S. Copyright Office Web site: www.loc.gov/copyright. Use the version that suits your product/protection needs best.

You can download application forms directly from the U.S. Copyright Office Web site. They are also in the process of making it possible to register on-line. Check to see if it's actually working when you're ready to register.

### "Pauper's Copyright"

You may have heard about a do-it-yourself, or "pauper's," copyright. This involves mailing a copy of your pattern to yourself, then putting the unopened but postmarked envelope in your safe or safety deposit box. Theoretically that's proof of date of publication. There's no guarantee it will carry water in court, however. To be safe, register with the copyright office.

## Correct Form

While not legally necessary, it's a good idea to notify readers that you claim a copyright to your original work by printing it on each page of your work. The copyright notice must include three elements:

- The copyright symbol (©) or the word "copyright"
- The year of first publication
- The name of the copyright owner

For patterns sold in some countries, the words "all rights reserved" must also appear

with the copyright notice. On my patterns, I include the notice "© 1999 Nancy Restuccia, All Rights Reserved" on each page (the year varies, of course).

## Fair Use

It is legal to copy and distribute copyrighted material without permission when it's for "fair use" purposes. Fair use is a judgement call (like most legal decisions). Basically it applies to situations such as quoting a short portion of a work in a review in order to give readers the flavor of the product. Fair use also allows distributors or shops to reproduce your pattern cover in a catalog or ad without getting your permission, in order to sell it.

Fair use does *not* include teachers making copies to distribute to students in commercial venues. This is another common misunderstanding (fair use only applies to teachers in academic and research settings). To learn more about fair use, check the resources listed at the end of this chapter.

## "Sharing" Patterns

The bad news for designers is, it's perfectly legal for your customer to lend their original copy of your pattern to a friend, or to sell it. As long as only the original pattern remains in circulation (i.e., they haven't made a second copy to keep for themselves), copyright law has not been violated.

Of course as the designer you may feel cheated when people borrow your work rather than buying their own copy. And the wise consumer understands that they need to support their favorite designers if they want them to stay in business. Nevertheless, it's not illegal to lend or sell patterns.

In legal terms, lending or selling a pattern is called "transferring ownership." The new owner has every right that the old owner did, which includes the right to use it for their own pleasure, as well as to transfer ownership back to the lender, or on to another person entirely, to sell it, etc.

## It's Amazing What People Ask!

Dear Nancy,

Today at our quilting club, we learned how to make your Humbag Bags™. They are so cute!

When I came home I mentioned them to an email friend who is in a charm-block swap, via email (seven ladies are in this charm swap). To make a long story short, this swapping group wanted copies of the directions for this bag. I started to make copies, and then noticed the "All Rights Reserved" on the bottom of the page, and that is why I am writing to you and asking permission for me to make six copies and send them to my group.


Dear Helen,

Thanks for writing to ask permission. I'm afraid I cannot give it.

I sell the pattern, and if you copy it and give it to your friends, you are denying me the profit that I deserve for the many, many hours of time and the considerable investment of money I have put into creating and printing and marketing the pattern. I hope you understand. If your friends want the pattern, they certainly can afford the $7 it costs to buy it for themselves, can't they?

I am a generous person, and glad to give permission to copy my work where it is warranted; but it doesn't seem to be a case of need from what you've described. I truly appreciate your respect for my rights as an author and publisher. To copy and distribute your copy of my pattern would be illegal (and actionable). Thanks for your personal integrity. Please let me know if I've misunderstood your situation,

Nancy Restuccia

"Sharing" only becomes a legal issue when copies of the original are made and then given away or sold. That's copyright infringement and thus is legally actionable.

There has been a good deal of press lately about people "sharing" patterns, particularly on the Internet. "Pattern Piggies" is one such group: an email list of folks who feel free to publish anything they purchase individually for use by the entire list of hundreds of partners-in-crime. (Yes, it is a crime. It's stealing, make no mistake about it. These are dishonest folk.) Several industry associations are taking aggressive action to educate consumers and to prosecute violators.

So, bottom line, when "sharing" means lending or selling an original, that's okay. When "sharing" means making additional copies from the original and passing the copies along, that's copyright infringement—whether or not any money changes hands, and no matter what the final form (i.e., photocopied, scanned, hand-written, etc.).

## Prosecuting Copyright Infringers

Going to court can be expensive. But there are also reasonable-cost options to prosecute someone for copyright infringement. Contact the Volunteer Lawyers for the Arts in your state to investigate whether you might qualify for *pro bono* (free) legal help. Industry organizations are also often interested in helping with copyright infringement cases.

## *Trademarks*

While a copyright protects your entire work, a trademark protects your name and/or slogan. (A "servicemark" protects the name/slogan of a service rather than a product.)

Trademarks differ from copyrights in that ownership is not necessarily established by registration. Trademarks can be registered; but ownership is earned by using and defending it. In a legal contest, most often the decision will be found for the company that has the greatest commercial interest (e.g., strongest name-recognition) in the trademark. For instance, even though Barbie Swanson was using the name "Barbie" long before Mattel came out with their doll, the court found in favor of Mattel and enjoined Barbie from using her own name in her business. Mattel had the greater commercial interest.

When registering a trademark, you need to do a little research to find out if there are any conflicts with your name. Many years ago I registered the business name "Words That Work!" for my writing business, and was told by the state licensing office that there was no other like it. A few years later I discovered that "Words At Work" was also operating in the state (indeed, just a few miles from my own office). I don't know which of us registered first, but the state saw no conflict (apparently they're happy to take both our fees). I was lucky that the other business was reputable and neither of us suffered from the inevitable confusion.

## Federal and State Trademarks

Trademarks can be registered federally and/or by state. These 51 registries are independent of each other. So if you register your trademark in your state, that does not guarantee that the trademark hasn't already been registered in another state or federally. Companies with a federal registration will claim that theirs takes precedence over state registrations; but state authorities will claim state-registered trademarks as their jurisdiction/priority for commerce within their state. Again, this is something that can only be decided in court.

Personally, I feel that registering trademarks by state is pretty worthless if you're engaged in "interstate commerce" (i.e., selling across state borders). It will cost you about $50 per state (filing fee) if you do it yourself; more if you hire someone to do it for you. And it doesn't guarantee anything outside of the state you register in. As a matter of fact, as far as I can tell, it doesn't even guarantee anything within that state—particularly if there's a federal trademark on file for a similar name.

In my opinion, the only reason to do a state registration is if you register all 50 states as well as federally. And it would take a pretty important trademark to justify that cost.

## Registering Your Trademark

As for copyrights, it is not necessary to register a trademark in order to own it. Long-term usage of an unregistered trademark can easily supercede a recently-registered user's right to use the mark if the former has a greater stake in ownership.

Personally, I consider federal trademark-registration to be an easy way to let others know that I've claimed the name. Most folks considering a name will check the Trademark Office's Web site to see what's been registered, and what's in the process of being registered (www.uspto.gov/web/menu/tm.html). So if you're on the list, other designers know to avoid a similar name. To me, federal trademark registration is a litigation-avoidance tactic rather than a claim device.

My personal bottom line: I don't register a trademark for each of my pattern names, unless they become particularly well known and thus important to protect. I do register my company name, however, since all my business hinges on its integrity. (I'm talking federal registration, not state-by-state.)

To register a state trademark, check with your Secretary of State for rules and forms. Federal trademarks can be registered on-line, from the U.S. Trademark Office Web site: http://www.uspto.gov/web/menu/tm.html. The current filing fee (as of 8/1/01) is $325. Or you can hire a lawyer to file for you.

Note that if you register incorrectly, you will be charged the entire registration fee anyway. That caveat was enough to scare me into hiring a lawyer (specializing in small-business issues) to do my first filing. Legal expenses added another $350 to my total cost, but it assured me that my application would be right the first time. And it let me know how to file the second time, without using a lawyer.

## Correct Form

There are two forms of trademark identification: ™ and ®. The first (™) may be used by anyone, whether or not the name is registered. The second (®) may only be used if the mark has been accepted as federally registered. (State registration does not qualify you to use the ® mark.)

Use the ™ symbol with all your pattern names, to indicate that you claim them as trademarks.

## Protecting Your Trademark

You must actively protect your trademark in order to keep it. One (in)famous example of a company that didn't go after infringers, and thus lost their trademark, is "aspirin." Once it was a brand name; now it's a generic name. That's why today, companies like Kimberly-Clark and Benetton Group are aggressive about protecting Kleenex and Rollerblade, respectively, as brand-specific rather than generic names.

If you become aware that someone is using your trademark, you must at least send a "cease and desist" letter in order to demonstrate that you are actively protecting your mark. If you just let it go, the courts may decide you don't care and either let it become generic or let someone else have the mark.

## "Cease and Desist" Letters

If you never get one, nor have to send one, consider yourself lucky. It's legal nastiness at its finest. If you get one, it will threaten you with all manner of retribution for compromising "their" trademark, including taking all your assets (home, cars, bank accounts) to satisfy their purported loss.

Don't panic! It's probably a form letter.

The good news is that it's costly for both parties to go to court (civil vs. criminal law), so my understanding is that most of these issues are settled amicably (or not) out of court.

The law allows more than one manufacturer to use a name, as long as there is no reasonable likelihood for consumer confusion. For instance, a craft pattern and an automotive part can use the same trademark; no consumer is going to get the two confused. (Still, the other trademark-owner may send you a cease-and-desist letter. It's his responsibility to do so, as legal proof that he's actively protecting the mark. Simply write back telling him (very nicely) that there is no reasonable possibility that consumers will confuse the two products. He may not stop hassling you until you get a lawyer to send essentially the same letter, but you might as well start with the low-cost option.)

If you learn that someone is violating your trademark, you can either send your own cease-and-desist letter, or for bigger/better impact, get your lawyer to do so. As mentioned, these are typically form letters so should not cost much.

Under no circumstances sign anything from anyone accusing you of trademark infringement without consulting your lawyer! Do not acknowledge that you are infringing on their trademark; do not offer to pay court costs; etc. This can be very serious/costly stuff. Hire a lawyer if you get deep into it.

## *Licensing Your Designs*

Customers may ask you for permission to make multiples of your pattern to sell at craft shows and the like. Personally, I allow customers to make a reasonable number of items to sell before I consider it a commercial venture. (See page 23, "Commercial-Production Disclaimer.") However, when the volume under discussion is significant, I think it's only fair that the designer be compensated for his/her design. A licensing agreement specifies the terms of that compensation.

Licensing agreements may be based on a charge per item sold, a percentage of sales, or a flat fee per year (or other time period). Often, 5–10% of profit is considered a reasonable licensing fee. Be sure to specify whether that's 5% of profit or of gross sales.

---

Dear X,

I'm delighted to sell you a license to make my Humbug Bag™ for sale. The fee is $25 for each 125 you make and sell. This license gives you permission to make and sell up to 500 bags over the course of the next 12 months.

This license also gives you permission to use my trademark (i.e., the name Humbug Bag™) in advertising and promotional materials used to sell your bags. You may also reproduce the gift tag included in the pattern to attach to each bag you sell.

A few legal considerations and common-sense caveats:

- Always use the ™ mark after the name "Humbug Bag" in your advertising/ signage (i.e., Humbug Bag™) (if mentioned more than once on a page, only the first usage needs the ™)

- You may not change the gift tag without prior review and approval from me

- You may not represent your bags in a way that most members of our culture would consider in bad taste (e.g., made up using pornographic fabric)

I wish you lots of success in your venture!

---

*Sample "friendly" licensing agreement (get your lawyer to write the non-friendly version)*

An important aspect of licensing is protecting your good name and reputation. A licensing agreement that I have used is reproduced above.

## *To Learn More*

### A Good Book

A book that I refer to constantly is *The Law [In Plain English] for Crafts*, by Leonard D. DuBoff (who *is* a lawyer). It's got lots of information on all sorts of legal issues.

### Web Sites

PubLaw Update is a free information service provided by the Publishing Law Center (sponsored by the law office of Lloyd L. Rich). To subscribe for periodic emailed newsletters, go to www.publaw.com and complete the subscription form. Or select articles to read from their archives at www.publaw.com/ legal.html

The Disaster Center has a great list of copyright and trademark links (www.disastercenter.com/copyrite.htm), including the U.S. legal code regarding copyright and Brad Templeton's useful and very readable "10 Big Myths About Copyright Explained."

Another site with great copyright links is www.bf.org/copylaw.htm

Sylvia Landman has written a nice article, "Copyright for Crafters & Quilters," that is available for free on her Web site; the link is at the bottom of her home page, www.Sylvias-studio.com.

U.S. Copyright Office Web site (www.loc.gov/copyright) provides both information and forms; soon they will offer on-line registration.

For some basic lessons on copyright and fair use, particularly as it pertains to cyberspace, check out: www.ssrn.com/update/ lsn/cyberspace/csl_lessons.html.

If you want to learn more about fair use with respect to teaching, check out www.utsystem.edu/OGC/IntellectualProperty/copypol2.htm#test. While it's written specifically for the University of Texas, it's good advice for almost anywhere.

For trademarks, the U.S. Trademark office has a searchable database so you can see if the names you are considering are already taken. You can also register a trademark on-line from their Web site: www.uspto.gov/web/menu/tm.html

For Canadian trademarks, check at www.strategis.ic.gc.ca/

# Appendices

## Appendix A:
# Two Other Ways to Get Published

You've bought this book, so you're interested in publishing your own patterns. Even so, you might decide after reading it that self-publishing involves way more than you want to, or are qualified, to take on.

If so, there are other ways to get published that don't require either the time or labor commitment that self-publishing does. Of course, the absolute financial return isn't as great either. But you have to do what you love, and if designing is your singular passion, it may well be worth the lesser financial return to sign over your babies to another publisher than to market your patterns yourself. (See sidebar by Jodie Davis for that perspective.)

Remember, that "extra" money you earn from self-publishing comes at the price of a bunch of time and effort. If that's not where you want to put your creative energy, don't! Some folks are cut out for running a business; others are "just" designers. Pursue your own passion. Life is too short to do stuff that doesn't make you happy.

## What Makes My Heart Sing?

*by Jodie Davis, quilt-book author and Rubber Duckie collector*

Often in my career I've been tempted to self-publish. In fact the latest incident was just today, when a publisher decided not to go with an idea I'm quite passionate about. But I know myself better and have not followed that path.

Why?

The question of self-publishing versus going with a publisher comes down to what you want to spend your time doing. From what I gather from those who do publish their own patterns and books, there is more money to be made doing so. They get 100% of the profit whereas I get a 10% royalty on my publisher's profits after costs.

And rightfully so. Just think about all the different hats the self-publisher must wear.

First, she wears the author hat, as do I. Add the chapeaux of designer, editor, illustrator, and production manager. Then back to the hat tree for the sales, marketing, publicity, and promotion head adornments. Don't forget distribution and the inevitable chasing of money. Oh, and warehousing the books and/or patterns. Personally, my knees are starting to buckle under the weight of all those hats!

Although I have a degree in business, most of those additional tasks don't appeal to me. I realized early on in my career that what I really like to do is design. Even wearing just the author hat, I spend a huge chunk of time every day dealing with the business end of things rather than playing with quilt designs in EQ and CorelDRAW and humming along with my Bernina—the things I love to do.

And that's exactly what anyone contemplating self-publishing needs to reflect upon: How do I envision my work days? How many hats do I want to wear? What makes my heart sing?

The two typical non-self-publishing arrangements are "fee for service" and "royalty." If one of these is better suited to your needs and resources than self-publishing, go for it. None is better or worse; they're just different.

## Fee for Service Arrangements

The lowest risk way to get your work published is with a fee-for-service arrangement, also called "freelancing." Simply stated, you sell your design (or words, or illustrations, or services) to a publisher for a flat fee, and the publisher takes care of getting your work to market. Magazines are the most common and plentiful venue for freelance assignments.

### Advantages and Disadvantages

The major advantages of fee-for-service:

- Virtually no investment required (in equipment, inventory, etc.)

- No long-term commitment (once your work is accepted, you're done)

- You know exactly how much money you'll make on the deal (you get paid even if it's a marketplace flop)

- You may get good "free" help writing and illustrating your design, making your work look far more professional than you might be capable of doing yourself

- You get potentially great exposure, depending on sales/circulation

The major disadvantages are:

- You give up control over your work (the editor can change things without asking)

- The pay tends to be low (sometimes just a free copy of the book or magazine in which your work is published)

- You don't get paid more if it's a huge success

- You may get no credit for your contribution (specify the credit you expect in the contract!)

- You may be giving up the right to re-use your work in the future (see "Regarding Rights" later in this appendix)

### A Few Tips

I've worked on a fee-for-service basis with many publishers over the years, and mostly it's been an absolute pleasure. The key to a good freelance relationship is clear communication. Be clear in telling the editor what you expect, and understand clearly what the editor needs. The editor usually has full discretion to decide if you have done the job that he/she assigned. If not, you may be asked to do it over or you may not be paid at all. Get all the essentials of your understanding in writing and upfront, to minimize misunderstandings and the potential for hard feelings later.

Two areas that are often contentious are samples and sidebars. An editor may expect you to supply samples for photography. If the samples you submit don't work with their layout, you may be asked to make additional samples in colors/fabrics that work better for them. Sample-making can be costly both in time and materials. Be clear going in who pays for what, and also who owns the samples after the article is published.

An editor may also request additional tips or a sidebar to accompany your article, even after you thought you were done. This is another good thing to discuss upfront.

A word about "kill fees." The editor may decide after you've written the article that he or she can't use it after all. There are a number of legitimate reasons this might occur. If it does, you should be paid a kill fee—a percentage of the original fee—for your efforts. Again, this is something that should be spelled out in your contract ahead of time.

### Increasing Your Chances

Increase your shot at getting published by putting yourself in the editor's shoes when pitching your idea. He/she is looking for articles that subscribers will love. Don't make the all-too-common mistake of telling an editor why *you* think your article deserves space in the magazine; tell her/him why you think the publication's *readers* will love it.

Educate yourself about each publication, then make your approach in terms that are specific to each one. Nobody is flattered to receive an obvious form letter. Demonstrate that you know:

- Who the target reader is (e.g., beginners? kids? avant garde artist-types?)

- What kind of articles they typically publish, and the way they're written (magazines have distinctive styles and formats)

- What they've published recently (don't pitch an article that's virtually identical to one they published in the last few months)

- How to spell the editor's name and his/her correct title (it's in the masthead)

## Where to Start

Begin by identifying the possibilities. You already know of several magazines from personal experience. Check the library (public as well as special collections at museums and guilds), bookstore, magazine stand, and in your favorite craft/sewing/quilt shops for others. Two additional places to look:

- *Writer's Market* published by F&W Publications each year (www.WritersMarket.com)

- Calls for entries advertised in magazines, newsletters, etc. (these often are for articles in books rather than magazines; Oxmoor House's annual *Greatest American Quilts* series is a prime example).

If you're not a regular reader of a promising publication, skim at least a year's worth of issues so you know what the editor is looking for.

Armed with that knowledge, decide which publications are the best match for your work. For instance, if your design is for a hand-crafted wedding favor, don't waste time sending it to *Raising Weasels for Fun and Profit* magazine. While editors generally claim to be looking for "something different," there's an uncanny sameness to what they publish issue to issue, year after year—a function, of course, of giving readers what they want.

Once you've figured out which publications are your best possibilities, find out how they like to be approached. Most editors like to receive proposals in writing. Some editors will accept them via email, though most still prefer old-fashioned wood pulp. Rarely does an editor like to receive a pitch by phone from someone he/she doesn't know.

Magazines vary in what they want to see in order to decide whether to offer a contract. One editor might want a fully written article; another might want to see the finished project; and many prefer to start with a "query letter" that describes your proposed article.

Most publications have "Writer's Guidelines" that detail what to send and the format in which it should be submitted. Request them by writing to the editor, or download them from the publication's Web site.

## *Royalty Arrangements*

A second alternative to self-publishing is to enter into a "royalty" agreement. This is very common in the book industry. (Appendix D lists a few pattern publishers that work on a royalty basis.) You contribute the concept and content and the publisher does the printing, warehousing, marketing, fulfillment, accounting, etc. You get paid a portion of the profits—called a royalty—based on actual sales.

## Advantages and Disadvantages

Major advantages of royalty arrangements:

- Virtually no investment required (in equipment, inventory, etc.)

- You may get good "free" help with writing and illustrating your design, making it look far more professional than you are capable of doing yourself

- If it's a hit in the marketplace, you earn more money for the same amount of work

- You may be able to parlay the prestige of having your name on the cover into other opportunities (e.g., teaching, lectures)

## Major disadvantages:

- Your income is determined by sales, which are influenced by the publisher's marketing efforts and distribution pipeline; but many publishers don't do much (be prepared to do a lot of marketing yourself)

- If it's a flop in the marketplace, you earn less money for the same amount of work

- Payment is delayed and can spread out over many years (publishers typically pay on a quarterly or biannual basis)

- Authors generally have no control over cover or title (considered part of marketing, which is the publisher's domain), and the editor can change the contents without conferring with the author

## More Than A Few Tips

Not surprisingly, clear communication is a key to success when setting up a royalty arrangement. A contract is essential; so is a lawyer who specializes in publishing law.

Publishers start with a standard contract that has been written with their best interests in mind. A lawyer can help you fine-tune and negotiate an agreement that meets your needs as well. One of the easiest items to adjust is usually the number of free copies you receive when the book is published.

Royalty percentages vary, although most are between 5% and 15%. Be sure you understand "percent of what?" before you sign a contract (e.g., 5% of gross sales may be better than 15% of net profits, depending on how each is calculated). Royalty percentages may rise after a certain number of copies are sold; for instance, 9% on the first 5,000 copies; 12% on the next 5,000; etc. And they often are lower for book-club and other specialty sales.

Publishers typically offer an "advance" to get you through the non-income-generating phase of your work (which, one hopes, will be confined to the time you spend writing it). Generally an advance is equal to what the publisher expects your first quarterly or biannual royalty payment to be. Note that this is an advance-against-income, i.e., a loan. You do have to pay it back. Be sure your contract specifies what happens if your book doesn't earn back the full advance (for instance, if you die before the manuscript is completed, or it simply bombs big-time; these are the wonderful kinds of contingencies that lawyers are trained to think of for you).

Publishers will sometimes offer a budget for supplies, sample-making, illustrations, photography, and the like. Again, this is negotiable and should be agreed-upon upfront and included in your written contract.

At what price will the publisher sell books to you? You may want to retail them yourself (e.g., at lectures, teaching gigs, or from a Web site), give copies as gifts, use them to promote sales, etc. As an author, are you just another vendor or do you get a discount?

What is the publisher's promotional-copy policy? If you identify a retailer who wants to consider stocking your book, will the publisher send a complimentary copy? Or does the retailer—or you—have to purchase it?

And have you heard about returns? Book publishing may be the only industry on earth where customers are allowed to return unsold merchandise months, even years, later and get a full credit. Returns are, of course, deducted from your royalties.

Finally, a brief note about marketing. Many authors are disappointed with the effort their publishers put into selling their book. It seems to be the nature of the beast today that publishers put most of their bucks and effort behind a few big sellers each season. If yours isn't one of them, well…. So be prepared to spend every bit as much time and effort promoting a book published by a commercial publisher as you would one you self-published.

That said, the publisher is on your team, so the marketing department should be open to promotional suggestions from an author. Suggestions made politely and that don't cost very much to implement will generally be met with gratitude and compliance.

# Getting Your Book Published

*by Lois Fletcher, designer, author, and teacher,*
*Peace By Piece Designs*

My first book happened quite by accident. Having been a pattern designer for less than a year, I was designing a series to market as a block-of-the-month. Feeling that most BOM patterns end up costing way too much (when you look at it realistically), I wanted to give my customers more for their money than just a single block every month. I decided to include instructions for another item that could be made from the same block pattern—ultimately giving the customer a house-full of matching decorator items when they finished.

After designing three of the patterns, I mentioned to my husband that I thought they had the potential to become a book instead of a pattern series. As is his custom, he matter-of-factly said, "So do it!"

Well, I had no idea how to write a book proposal, much less a book, but still I decided to investigate by searching the Internet for information.

I found a couple of useful Web sites, both of which mentioned a book by Michael Larsen entitled *How to Write a Book Proposal*. I purchased the book. It was geared toward non-fiction, but not specifically toward quilt books. So I took the information that I thought applied and put together a proposal, still not certain that what I had done was the correct way to do it. But hey, nothing ventured, nothing gained, right? As was recommended in the Larsen book, I also suggested three sequels to the manuscript I had outlined in the proposal.

I then went through my personal quilt-book library and made a list of potential publishers. I put them in priority order, with the ones I considered my top choices at the beginning. I planned to start at the top of my list and work my way down as I received my rejections.

Little did I know that my first submission would be accepted! Not only that, but they expressed an interest in all three sequels I mentioned as well.

My first book, *The Quilter's Home: Fall,* will be published by Martingale & Company (a.k.a. That Patchwork Place) in spring of 2002.

I suppose if I was pressed to offer any advice to a beginner, it would be: Follow your instincts, and don't let inexperience get in the way of your success. You may think that you don't know what you are doing, but you will never know if you don't try.

The best commercial publishers have a well-developed and carefully nurtured distribution pipeline that automatically sells books for you. These connections often include book clubs, which can move a lot of volume.

## Increasing Your Chances

The best way to increase your shot at getting a book published is to put yourself in the publisher's shoes. Know their audience, their style, and their niche in the marketplace. Then position your concept as filling a need in their line-up—one that will be hugely appealing and make lots of money.

And of course, know whom the appropriate editor is to send your idea to, as well as their correct title and how to spell their name.

## Where to Start

Begin by identifying the possibilities. Notice who publishes books that seem to be a good fit with your concept. Check resources such as F&W Publications' annual *Writer's Market* (www.WritersMarket.com). Then narrow the possibilities to one best match. (I won't discuss "multiple submissions" here; suffice it to say, it is generally considered proper to send a proposal to one publisher at a time.)

Most book editors want a proposal as the first step. A book proposal usually includes:

- An outline of content

- Who you think your book will appeal to (including demographics, size, revenue-potential, and how to reach that market)

- Why you think the title will sell

- Often, a sample chapter to demonstrate your writing ability

- And finally, the reason why you're the best person on earth to write this book.

Publishers vary in how formal and how complete a book proposal needs to be. If you're an established writer, you may be able to get away with little more than a good cover letter and list of projects you've already done. If you're trying to break in as an author, you may be required to demonstrate not only the merits of your concept, but also your ability to write/illustrate clearly, and your perseverance to see the project through to completion.

## *Regarding Rights*

What do I mean by "rights"? Rights detail how the publisher is able to use your work in return for the payment you've agreed upon. Rights vary widely among publishers, and even among publications within a publisher's stable.

## Magazine Rights

Many magazines purchase "first North America" rights: the privilege of being the first to publish your original work in North America. With first N.A. rights, you are guaranteeing that the work has not been previously published, and giving the publisher permission to publish and profit from your work for a specified period of time (generally three months to a year from the publication date). After that time, ownership of the work reverts to you, to self-publish or to re-sell as you wish (except that, by definition, you can never again sell "first rights"; subsequent re-sales would be "second rights," "third," etc.).

Some publishers demand "all rights," which means they can publish your work in whatever form they want, forever. They may publish it in an anthology; they may publish it on their Web site; they may publish it years later in an anniversary issue as a golden oldie; etc. When you sell all rights, you are agreeing that you will never publish or resell that design/article again.

Selling all rights may not be as bad as it sounds. While the publisher owns the exact design, samples, words, and illustrations you sold them, you can write a new article using the same concept but creating something different with it. You then can resell or self-publish that reslanted work.

For example, I sold an article to a magazine detailing how to make a slash-fabric scarf. While I can't sell the same words or project or samples ever again, I can write a different article or pattern that tells, say, how to make a slash-fabric vest using the same basic techniques, and then sell that reslanted piece to another publisher.

The issue of rights is complex. It's always a good idea to either check with a lawyer or to do some serious reading on the topic before signing contracts.

## Issues Peculiar to Book Publishing

Be clear who owns the rights to your book when the publisher decides to let it go out of print. Ideally, all rights should revert to the author, so that you can either sell it to another publisher or use the material yourself.

Many books are written as a result of an author having established a good reputation as a designer/publisher first. These types of books may include designs that have been previously published. If you've sold "all rights" previously, you will need to obtain written permission to re-use the designs and/or images in the book. If you wish to include designs/instructions that you are currently self-publishing (e.g., as patterns), you may be asked to discontinue their publication for the lifetime of the book. Again, be clear before you sign anything what rights you are granting the publisher.

## Employment Status and Rights

This is a complicated topic, but absolutely one that you need to consider before you work with a publisher because it determines not only who owns your work, but also things like pay and benefits. I can only scratch the surface here; please check with a lawyer and/or accountant to define your particular situation.

Basically, there are three types of work relationships: employee, independent contractor, and work-for-hire. To summarize very briefly (and again, check with your lawyer for an opinion on your particular situation):

- If you're classified as an employee, you are entitled to employee benefits, and your work is the property of your employer.

- If you're not an employee, the situation becomes more murky. The legal alternatives are "independent contractor" and "work for hire." An independent contractor owns and maintains rights to his/her work; in a work-for-hire situation, the company who has hired the work owns the rights and may do with it as they please (upon payment of the agreed-upon fee).

The IRS has very stringent requirements to differentiate between these three types of employment relationships, many of which center on who is controlling/directing performance of the work and who is at risk. You can see the IRS's "Twenty Common Factors" test at www.contingentlaw.com/IRS20.htm

Check with your lawyer and/or accountant to be sure you stay on the right side of the law, and also to maintain the rights that are important to you.

# Appendix B:
# Editors

This is by no means an exhaustive list of editors; rather, it is a handful of people I know and would trust editing my own work. Please contact them directly for their qualifications, experience, and prices. Addresses are in the U.S.A. unless otherwise noted.

**Anne Brennan**
Allegro Communications
10375 Sandiford Drive
Richmond, BC, V7E 5S6, Canada
email: abrennan@telus.net
phone: 604-271-5172
fax: 604-275-2123

**Rosalie Cooke**
3567 Benton St., PMB 430
Santa Clara, CA 95051
email: Rosekcooke@aol.com
phone/fax: 408-249-0451
Web: www.artwearnews.com

**Barbara Herbert**
725 S. High Street
Sebastopol, CA 95472-4315
email: sewing@sonic.net
phone: 707-824-8077
fax: 707-824-8078

**Susan Huxley**
Sew'n Tell Studio
67 N. 4th St.
Easton, PA, 18042-3530
email: huxley@ptd.net
phone: 610-252-0299
Web: www.sewntellstudio.com

**Janet F. O'Brien**
3656 Cherbourg Way
Marietta, GA 30062-4289
email: janetfobrien@mindspring.com
phone: 770-971-2675
fax: 770-565-6324

**Barbara Weiland**
6835 SW Capitol Hill Road, #34
Portland, OR, 97219
email: barbaraweiland@aol.com
phone: 503-892-8265

# Appendix C:
# Printers

Again, this is not an exhaustive list. Chances are, there are dozens of printers in or near your town that might be better to work with than a long-distance supplier. But it's worth checking around for prices and service; both vary significantly from shop to shop.

**McCall Pattern Company**
Commercial Printing
615 McCall Road
Manhattan, KS 66502
email: daveh@comprt.mccall.com
toll-free phone: 800-255-2762
(for tissue-paper patterns, newsprint instruction sheets, and envelopes; 1,000 minimum)

**MegaColor**
Various studio locations around the country; printing facility is in Florida
toll-free phone: 888-565-5512
Web: www.megacolor.com
(color printing only)

**Palmer Printing**
Attn: Gloria/Crafts Department
P.O. Box 1575
St. Cloud, MN 56302
toll-free phone: 800-336-3504
local phone: 320-252-0033
fax: 320-252-9547
Web: www.palmerprinting.com

**Timm Enterprises**
9268 Narcissus Road
St. Joseph, MN 56374
email: dtimm@spacestar.net
toll-free phone: 888-363-8298
fax: 320-363-8293

**Tri-State Printing**
157 N. Third Street
Steubenville, OH 43952
toll-free phone: 800-642-1166
local phone: 740-283-3686
fax: 740-282-9351

# Appendix D:
# Pattern Publishers

While there are lots of book publishers, there are very few pattern publishers. Which is one of the reasons many designers publish their own patterns.

**Indygo Junction**
P.O. Box 30238
Kansas City, MO 64112
email: indygo@qni.com
Web: www.indygojunctioninc.com

**Make It Easy Sewing & Crafts**
A QuiltWoman.com company
Attn: Ann Anderson
26540 Canada Way
Carmel, CA 93923-9551
email: ann@quiltwoman.com
phone: 831-624-0700
Web: www.make-it-easy.com
   and www.quiltwoman.com

**Seams To Be**
Attn: Rae Jean Goodwin
P.O. Box 1845
Magalia, CA 95954
530-873-2670
email: like2quilt@aol.com
Web: www.seams2be.com

The following is a content and production service rather than a publisher. The staff of seasoned professionals can help with any or all of the following: development, photography, illustration, editing (of copy, illustrations, and patterns), layout, and printing.

**Sew'n Tell Studio**
Attn: Susan Huxley
67 N. 4th St.
Easton, PA, 18042-3530
email: huxley@ptd.net
phone: 610-252-0299
Web site: www.sewntellstudio.com

# Appendix E:
# Publications & Organizations

Following are some good sources for industry information.

*American Quilt Retailer*, published bimonthly by Susan Fuquay, P.O. Box 172876, Arlington, TX 76003-2876, 817-478-6790, email SFuquay@aol.com

American Sewing Guild (ASG) and its quarterly newsletter, *Notions*, 9660 Hillcroft, Suite 516, Houston, TX 77096, 713-729-3000, www.asg.org

*Art You Wear*, quarterly newsletter published by Rosalie Cooke, 3567 Benton St. PMB 430, Santa Clara, CA 95051, email Rosekcooke@aol.com, 408-249-0451, www.artwearnews.com

Association of Crafts & Creative Industries (ACCI), P.O. Box 3388, Zanesville, OH 43702-3388, 740-452-4541, www.accicrafts.org

Canadian Craft & Hobby Association (CCHA), #24, 1410 40th Avenue NE, Calgary, AB T2E 6L1, 403-291-0559 (ext. 22), www.cdncraft.org

*CNA*, published monthly by Krause Publications, 700 East State Street, Iola, WI 54990, 800-258-0929, www.krause.com/crafts/cn/

*The Crafts Report*, published monthly, P.O. Box 1992, Wilmington, DE 19899-1992, 800-777-7098, www.craftsreport.com

*Craft Supply*, published bimonthly by Krause Publications (address with *CNA* listing)

*Craftrends*, published monthly by Primedia Enthusiast Group, 741 Corporate Circle, Golden, CO 80401, 847-647-0756; on-line at www.craftrends.com/news.cfm

The Fabric Shop Network (FabShopNet) association and newsletter published bimonthly by Laurie Harsh, P.O. Box 4128, Vancouver, WA 98662, 360-892-6500, email fabshopnet@aol.com, www.fabshopnet.com

Hobby Industries Association (HIA), P.O. Box 348, Elmwood Park, NJ 07407, 201-794-1133, www.hobby.org

Home Sewing Association (HSA), 1350 Broadway, Suite 1601, New York, NY 10018, 212-714-1633, www.sewing.org

National Craft Association (NCA) and free newsletter, 2012 E. Ridge Road, Suite 120, Rochester, NY 14622-2434, 800-715-9594, 716-266-5472, www.craftassoc.com

*The Professional Quilter*, published quarterly by Morna McEver Golletz, 22412 Rolling Hill Lane, Laytonsville, MD 20882, 301-482-2345, email ProQuilter@aol.com, www.professionalquilter.com

VDTA/SDTA (Vacuum Dealers/Sewing Dealers Trade Assiation) and their three monthly magazines: *Sewing Professional/Round Bobbin, Embroidery Professional, and Quilting Professional*, 2724 2nd Avenue, Des Moines, IA 50313, 800-367-5651, www.vdta.com

# Appendix F:
# Shows & Expos

There are dozens of trade and consumer shows every month; this list is just a sampling. Trade publications and associations often publish more complete lists, for instance the one at www.craftassoc.com/confer.html.

## TRADE SHOWS

Association of Crafts & Creative Industries (ACCI), P.O. Box 3388, Zanesville, OH 43702-3388, 740-452-4541, www.accicrafts.org

Canadian Craft & Hobby Association (CCHA), #24, 1410 40th Avenue NE, Calgary, AB T2E 6L1, 403-291-0559 (ext. 22), www.cdncraft.org

Hobby Industries Association (HIA), P.O. Box 348, Elmwood Park, NJ 07407, 201-794-1133, www.hobby.org

Home Sewing Association (HSA), 1350 Broadway, Suite 1601, New York, NY 10018, 212-714-1633, www.sewing.org

International Quilt Market, sponsored by Quilts, Inc., 7660 Woodway, Suite 550, Houston, TX 77063, 713-781-6864, www.quilts.com

## CONSUMER EXPOS

American Quilter's Society (AQS), P.O. Box 3290, Paducah, KY 42002-3290, www.AQSquilt.com

American Sewing Expo, (Novi, MI) 1385 Clyde Rd., Highland, MI 48357, 248-889-3111, www.americansewingexpo.com

Creative Sewing & Needlework Festival, 15 Wertheim Court, Suite 502, Richmond Hill, ON, Canada L4B 3H7, 905-709-0100 or 800-291-2030, www.csnf.com

International Quilt Festival, sponsored by Quilts, Inc., 7660 Woodway, Suite 550, Houston, TX 77063, 713-781-6864, www.quilts.com

Mid-Atlantic Quilt Festival/Wearable Art Festival/Fiber Arts Fair (Williamsburg, VA), Mancuso, Inc., P.O. Box 667, New Hope, PA 18938, www.quiltfest.com

Original Sewing & Craft Expo, produced by MS Productions, Inc., 26612 Center Ridge Road, Westlake, OH 44145, 440-899-6300 or 800-699-6309, www.sewncraftexpo.com

Pacific International Quilt Festival (Santa Clara, CA), Mancuso, Inc., P.O. Box 667, New Hope, PA 18938, www.quiltfest.com

Road to California, 5436 F Arrow Highway, Montclair CA 91763-1611, 909-946-0020 or 877-762-3222, www.road2ca.com

Sewing & Stitchery Expo, sponsored by Washington State University in Pierce County, Western Washington Fairgrounds, 110 9th Ave SW, Puyallup, Washington 98371, www.sewexpo.com

# Appendix G:

# Distributors

A few to get you started:

**Aptex, Inc.**
1205 Andover Park West
Seattle, WA 98188
206-575-0560

**Brewer Sewing Supplies**
197 Evergreen
Springfield, TN 37172
615-384-1383
www.brewersewing.com

**Checker Distributors**
400-B W. Dussel Drive
Maumee, OH 43537-1731
419-893-3636
www.checkerdist.com

**House of White Birches**
306 East Parr Road
Berne, IN 46711
219-589-4000
www.whitebirches.com

**Peterson-Arne**
3690 West First Avenue
Eugene, OR 97402
541-684-5078

**The Pattern Peddlers**
701 Walsen Avenue
Walsenberg, CO 81089
719-738-7271

**QuiltWoman.com**
26540 Canada Way
Carmel, CA 93923
1-877-454-7967
www.quiltwoman.com

**Quilter's Resource Inc.**
P.O. Box 148850
Chicago, IL 60614
773-278-5695
www.quiltersresource.com

**Quilter's Rule International**
817 Mohr Avenue
Waterford, WI 53185
800-343-8671
www.quiltersrule.com

**R&Z/The Quiltworks**
1055 E. 79th Street
Minneapolis, MN 55420
952-854-1460
www.r-and-z.com

**United Notions**
13795 Hutton Drive
Dallas, TX 75234
1-800-468-4209
www.unitednotions.com

# Appendix H:
# Catalogs

Most of these folks will request/demand distributor pricing. Assuming they can meet your minimum (for me it was four dozen patterns, mixed titles okay), I recommend that you give it to them, even if they're not distributors in the strictest sense (though many are).

*Connecting Threads*/Crafts Americana Group
13118 N.E. 4th Street
Vancouver, WA 98684
360-260-8900
www.connectingthreads.com

Home-Sew
1825 W. Market Street
Bethlehem, PA 18018
800-344-4739
www.homesew.com

House of White Birches
306 East Parr Road
Berne, IN 46711
219-589-4000
www.whitebirches.com

Keepsake Quilting, Inc.
Route 25B
Centre Harbor, NH 03226-8346
603-243-8148
www.keepsakequilting.com

Patterncrafts, Inc.
3919 Van Teylingen Drive
Colorado Springs, CO 80917
719-522-0611
www.patterncrafts.com

Quilter's Warehouse
107 N. Second Street
P.O. Box 458
Cissna Park, IL 60924
(815) 457-2867
www.quilterswarehouse.com

*Quilts & Other Comforts*/Clotilde, Inc.
4301 N. Federal Highway, Suite 200
Fort Lauderdale, FL 33308-5209
954-491-2889
www.quiltson-line.com

Sew Baby!
313 N. Mattis, Suite 116
Champaign, IL 61826
217-398-1440
www.sewbaby.com

# Appendix I:
# Suppliers

Most of the supplies you need will be easy to find locally. Following are sources for a few items that might be a bit more difficult.

### DISPLAY FIXTURES, ACRYLIC

Jule-Art, Inc., P.O. Box 91748, Albuquerque, NM, 87199, 505-344-8433, www.jule-art.com

### DISPLAY FIXTURES, GENERAL

Palay Display Industries, Inc., 5250 West 73rd Street, Edina, MN 55439, 612-835-7171

### FLOORING (INTERLOCKING CARPET SQUARES)

Popcorn International, Inc., 10 Meadowpoint, Aliso Viejo, CA 92656, phone: 949-362-8445, fax: 603-954-0354, toll-free order phone: 1-888-809-6633, email: service@wondermat.com, www.wondermat.com

### NCR FORMS

goprinting.com, 1560 Superior Avenue, Suite A-3, Costa Mesa, CA 92627, 949-548-5455, www.goprinting.com

### NEWSPRINT IN SHEETS

ABC School Supply, www.abcschoolsupply.com, 800-669-4222

### PLASTIC ZIP-LOCK BAGS (2 MIL. WITH VENT HOLES)

G.T. Bag Company, 27-J Commercial Blvd., Novato, CA 94949; www.gtbag.com; 800-735-3950

Supply Line, P.O. Box 150, Kurten, TX 77862; 800-537-2067

### SHIPPING SUPPLIES

Chiswick, Inc., 33 Union Avenue, Sudbury, MA 01776-2267, 800-225-8708

Quilt Corporation, 100 Schelter Road, Lincolnshire, IL 60069-3621, 800-789-1331

Uline, 2200 S. Lakeside Drive, Waukegan, IL 60085, 800-295-5571, www.uline.com

# Appendix J:
# Resources & References

## BOOKS

*The Law [In Plain English] for Crafts*, by Leonard D. DuBoff, ©1999, Allworth Press

*Names That Sell: How to Create Great Names for Your Company, Product, or Service*, by Fred Barrett, ©1995, Alder Press (to order from the publisher call 503-246-7983 or email alder@teleport.com)

*On Writing Well*, by William Zinsser, 6th edition, ©1998, HarperCollins College Publishers

*Pricing Guidelines for Arts & Crafts: Successful, Professional Crafters Share Their Pricing Strategies to Help You Set Profitable Prices for Your Art*, by Sylvia Landman, ©2000, www.Sylvias-studio.com

*Quilter's Traveling Companion*, edited by Audrey Swales Anderson, published every two years by Chalet Publishing (32 Grand Avenue, Manitou Springs, CO 80829), 719-685-5041

*Type It Right! the little black book for your computer*, by Anita Stumbo, 2nd edition, ©1997, Addax Publishing Group

*Writer's Market*, published annually by F&W Publications, 1507 Dana Ave., Cincinnati, OH 45207, www.WritersMarket.com

## WEB SITES

www.onlinewbc.org/docs/market/ for marketing information (sponsored by the Small Business Association)

www.parapublishing.com information about self-publishing books, but much of it is applicable to patterns

www.prweb.com PRWeb, a free on-line service that delivers your press release to lots of recipients

www.quiltuniversity.com on-line courses on a variety of topics, including business issues (for instance, Sylvia Landman on pricing and Patti Anderson on using quilting software)

www.reallybig.com & www.bignosebird.com for information about building a Web site

Web sites about copyright and trademarks are listed at the end of Chapter 15

# Appendix K:
# Sidebar Contributors

The following folks were kind enough to share their expertise in these pages. I personally recommend the products and services offered by every one of them. Please contact them directly to purchase patterns, books, subscriptions, or to inquire about teaching, publishing, and other services.

**Ann Anderson** has been quilting for 26 years, and has been a distributor of quilting pattern for the last three. QuiltWoman.com was born when Ann started publishing her own patterns and recognized a need for a distributor that focused on emerging/new designers. In addition to being a distributor, Ann is now moving into publishing. She currently publishes four pattern lines: her own, Designs From Norway, Another Pat's Patterns, and Make It Easy Sewing & Crafts. *Publish Your Patterns!* is her first book-publishing venture.

Prior to opening QuiltWoman.com, Ann spent 23 years in sales and marketing in the computer industry. Ann's education, of course, had nothing to do with her occupation; her academic degrees are in biology. Her passions, though, have remained constant over the years: art, color, and fabrics.

> QuiltWoman.com
> Make It Easy Sewing & Crafts
> 26540 Canada Way, Carmel, CA
> 93923-9551
> Toll-free order phone: 877-454-7967
> Fax: 831-624-7132
> Email: ann@quiltwoman.com
> Web: www.quiltwoman.com
> and www. make-it-easy.com

**Patti R. Anderson** (no relation to Ann) is a quilt teacher and pattern designer from West Virginia. She has been quiltmaking for 14+ years and recently began self-publishing patterns under the name Patchpieces. She is a faculty member at QuiltUniversity.com, where she teaches on-line classes about Electric Quilt software and quilting classes using her own designs.

Patti Anderson,
Patchpieces, 509 Pike Street, Shinnston,
WV 26431-1407
Phone: 304-592-0508 or 304-592-5476
Email: patti@patchpieces.com
Web: www.patchpieces.com

**Rosalie Cooke** has a passion for patterns, especially those suited to wearable art. She has been sewing for centuries yet still gets breathless over an original style or a great, new twist on an idea. Another love is sorting through instructions that need help—whether writing pattern reviews for her newletter, editing books, or editing patterns.

*Art You Wear* newsletter, 3567 Benton St.
PMB #430, Santa Clara, CA 95051
Phone/fax: 408-249-0451
Email: Rosekcooke@aol.com
Web: www.artwearnews.com

**Jodie Davis** is a designer, teacher, and author of a dozen crafts books that range from home decorating to cloth dolls to teddy-bear making to quilting. She is well-known for her innovative techniques—well-demonstrated in her two latest quilting books, *Paper Pieced Curves* and *Raw Edge Appliqué*. She is also well-known for her Rubber Duckie collection. She was recently photographed in the bathtub with them for the Atlanta evening news.

Email: jodie@iejodie.com
Web: www.iejodie.com

**Beth Ferrier** has been a quilter since the dark ages and a teacher since the dawn of time. She now manages to publish patterns and books, write for magazines, parent four teenaged boys, and captivate her husband of 25 years—all in a 24-hour day. [Ed. note: She's also quite the comic… and has great hair!] Her first book, *Out of the Cupboard and Onto the Bed: Practically Free Quilts From Your Fabric Stash*, was published in 2001.

> Beth Ferrier
> Applewood Farm Publications, 3655 Midland Road, Saginaw, MI 48603
> Phone: 989-799-6973
> Email: quilting@applewd.com
> Web: www.applewoodfarmquilts.com

**Lois Fletcher** is an award-winning quilter, designer, author, and teacher. Her first book, *The Quilter's Home: Fall*, will be published by Martingale & Co. in spring of 2002.

> Peace By Piece Designs, 108 E. Ila Street, Elgin, TX 78621
> Phone: 512-281-3470
> Email: LFletcher@PeacebyPieceDesigns.com
> Web: www.PeaceByPieceDesigns.com

**Mary-Jo McCarthy** started her company in 1992 with 24 patterns she purchased from another designer. Her first corporate office was in her home: a room the size of a broom closet. Today, Southwest Decoratives offers patterns from over 20 designers (including over 100 of Mary-Jo's own designs) and carries almost 2,000 bolts of fabric. Mary-Jo opened a retail store in 2001, to complement her existing mail-order catalog and Web-based businesses.

The secret of her success? Mary-Jo explains that she picked a theme (Southwest Decoratives), carved out a niche, and took her time building the business from a broom closet to a 2,500-square-foot retail shop plus a thriving Web business. She has been advertising regularly since the very beginning, and continues to increase the size of her ads as well as the number of publications she advertises in every year.

> Southwest Decoratives, 5711 Carmel Ave. NE, Suite B, Albuquerque, NM 87113
> Phone: 800-530-8995 or 505-821-7400
> Email: swd@swdecoratives.com
> Web: www.swdecoratives.com

**Susan Purney-Mark** and **Daphne Greig** own Patchworks Studio, based in Victoria, British Columbia, Canada. They have been in business since 1996, when Susan and Daphne formed a partnership to market their quilt designs. Patchworks Studio has become Canada's foremost quilters' Web site with over 8,000 hits monthly. Their three annual series—Millennium Quilt, Club Medallion and Blooms and Bouquets—have been made by quilters around the world. Susan and Daphne are also co-authors of *Quilted Havens*, published by the American Quilter's Society in 2000.

> Patchworks Studio, 2552 Eastdowne Rd., Victoria, BC, Canada V8R 5P9
> Phone: 250-595-4411
> Fax: 250-595-4377
> Email: patchworkstudio@home.com
> Web: www.patchworkstudio.com

# Index

# Order Form

**Call** toll free:
1-877-454-7967

**Fax** this form to:
1-831-624-7132

**Mail** this form to:
QuiltWoman.com
26540 Canada Way
Carmel, CA, USA
93923-9551

**Online** ordering:
www.make-it-easy.com

| | Qty. | Cost ea. | Total cost |
|---|---|---|---|
| **Book:** Publish Your Patterns! How to Write, Print, and Market Your Designs, by Nancy Restuccia | | $19.95 | |
| **Patterns by Nancy Restuccia:** KinderKakes™ | | $ 7 | |
| BridalBakes™ | | 7 | |
| FlapHappy™ | | 7 | |
| Pocket Scribbler™ | | 7 | |
| Humbug Bag™ | | 7 | |
| Jambalaya™ | | 9 | |
| Rumbleford™ | | 9 | |
| Subtotal | | | |
| Sales tax (CA residents add 7% to subtotal) | | | |
| Shipping:      In the U.S.:  $3 for Book Rate $4.50 for Priority Mail Canada & Mexico: $5 for AirMail Letter Post $8 for Global Priority Other non-U.S. destinations: $10 for Global Priority | | | |
| Total enclosed (U.S. funds only, please) | | | |

Name _____

Address _____

City _____ State _____ ZIP _____

Telephone _____ Country _____

Email address _____

| Payment Method* | Special Instructions: |
|---|---|
| Credit Card ☐ Check or M.O. ☐ | |

*International orders by credit card only

Credit Card Type:  VISA  MC  AMEX    Number _____ Exp. Date _____

Billing Address _____ City _____ ZIP_____
(If different from above)

Signature _____ Date _____

# Order Form

**Call** toll free:
1-877-454-7967

**Fax** this form to:
1-831-624-7132

**Mail** this form to:
QuiltWoman.com
26540 Canada Way
Carmel, CA, USA
93923-9551

**Online** ordering:
www.make-it-easy.com

|  | Qty. | Cost ea. | Total cost |
|---|---|---|---|
| **Book:** Publish Your Patterns! How to Write, Print, and Market Your Designs, by Nancy Restuccia |  | $19.95 |  |
| **Patterns by Nancy Restuccia:**<br>KinderKakes™ |  | $ 7 |  |
| BridalBakes™ |  | 7 |  |
| FlapHappy™ |  | 7 |  |
| Pocket Scribbler™ |  | 7 |  |
| Humbug Bag™ |  | 7 |  |
| Jambalaya™ |  | 9 |  |
| Rumbleford™ |  | 9 |  |
| Subtotal |  |  |  |
| Sales tax (CA residents add 7% to subtotal) |  |  |  |
| Shipping:        In the U.S.:  $3 for Book Rate<br>$4.50 for Priority Mail<br>Canada & Mexico: $5 for AirMail Letter Post<br>$8 for Global Priority<br>Other non-U.S. destinations: $10 for Global Priority |  |  |  |
| Total enclosed (U.S. funds only, please) |  |  |  |

Name _____

Address _____

City _____  State _____  ZIP _____

Telephone _____  Country _____

Email address _____

| Payment Method*<br><br>Credit Card ☐<br>Check or M.O. ☐ | Special Instructions: |
|---|---|

*International orders by credit card only

Credit Card Type:  VISA   MC   AMEX    Number_____  Exp. Date _____

Billing Address _____  City _____  ZIP _____
         (If different from above)

Signature_____  Date_____